MW00622188

TARGET
LEADERSHIP

TARGET
LEADERSHIP

MANAGERS MANAGE

LEADERS INFLUENCE

TARGET LEADERS INSPIRE

JEFF "ODIE" ESPENSHIP

Switches Safe, Inc.
Ocala, FL

© 2013 Jeff "Odie" Espenship

All rights reserved. No part of this publication may be reproduced, stored in retrieval system, or transmitted in any form or by any means electronic, mechanical, photocopying, recording or otherwise, without the prior written permission of the publisher.

Published by
Switches Safe, Inc.
Ocala, FL

Publisher's Cataloging-in-Publication Data
Espenship, Jeff.

Target leadership : managers manage, leaders influence, target leaders inspire / Jeff "Odie" Espenship. – Ocala, FL : Switches Safe, Inc., 2013.

p. ; cm.

ISBN13: 978-0-9860369-0-3

1. Leadership. 2. Life change events. 3. Airplanes—Piloting—United States. Espenship family. I. Title.

BF637.L4 E77 2013
158.4—dc23   2013933299

FIRST EDITION

Project coordination by Jenkins Group, Inc.
www.BookPublishing.com

Interior design by Brooke Camfield

Printed in the United States of America
17   16   15   14   13   •   5   4   3   2   1

DEDICATION

This book is dedicated to the memory of my brother
John Michael Espenship, and to his surviving sons, Zachary and Alan.

Jeff and John.

CONTENTS

ACKNOWLEDGMENTS

Although this book is intended to help facilitate a strong safety program within companies, many of the principles can also be applied to family dynamics. I can thank my three beautiful children, Joellen, Michael, and Kai, for teaching me how to be a parent. Joellen and Michael spearheaded the project, since they were born to me in my youth, when I only thought I knew everything. As I led them, they taught me. Nearly 20 years later, Kai has brought up the rear. With joy, we experience our exciting world through his eyes, and I am glad that he has been born to a wiser and more patient and thoughtful dad. I expect that as I lead him, he will teach me just as much as Joellen and Michael did. I hope to pass on what I have learned to these children who will soon be among the Target Leaders of their generation.

I also benefited from good parenting. I remember the human resources person standing in front of our group of 30 airline new-hire pilots and saying, "Congratulations! In order to hire you, we screened more than 1,000 pilot applications and picked 100 of those applicants to interview. Of those 100, we picked you 30 because not only are you qualified to fly for this airline but also you had great parenting." When I think back to the rigorous three-day interview process, I remember that many of the questions centered on social intelligence and people skills. In other words, all applicants who interviewed for the job were actually hired when they walked in the door. How well each pilot applicant played in the sandbox with others was *the deciding factor* as to whether he or she was offered a job at the end of the multiday interview.

Looking back, I see the truth in this. I have had great coaches, teachers, and mentors in my life, but none has taught me life skills better than my mom. She has been my inspiration and my main supporter for all that I have accomplished. As I finished each chapter of this book, I would send it to her and she would pore over it line by line and offer her gentle wisdom and thoughtful comments. Along the way, we cried together and laughed together. I'll be forever grateful to my mom for helping me become a better person every day.

For all her help, the net proceeds from this book will go directly to her for all she does for me and for others.

Foreword

Target Leaders Pursue Perfection to Achieve Excellence

—◁◦◦◦▷—

A pilot lives in a world of perfection, or not at all.

—Richard S. Drury

—◁◦◦◦▷—

That quote from Richard Drury is the very reason that writing this book has been such a struggle for me. I want it to be perfect, but it isn't. I have been trained to pursue perfection. The *pursuit of perfection* for Irish writer and poet Oscar Wilde was the proper placement of one comma. He wrote, "I have spent most of the day putting in a comma and the rest of the day taking it out." I was chatting with the chef at a fine restaurant in Atlanta about serving the perfect dish. He said, "The difference between an excellent dish and the perfect dish is three grains of salt, and I have to accept it." His words hold a lot of truth. I, too, have to accept this book not as perfect but as a reflection of my best effort. Giving my best, with an eye toward improvement next time, is all that I can ask of myself. That is perfect enough for me.

Where has the pursuit of perfection gone? We've seen, in recent years, how quick fixes, shortcuts, and skirting the rules can have disastrous effects, whether in business, engineering, manufacturing, or elsewhere in life. Pick up any newspaper or log on to any news site on the web and you can see the results of those actions playing out every single day.

Much of this book is about getting back to basics and staying grounded in the fundamentals, such as: Reflecting inward first. Being accountable, not held accountable. Listening to understand. Avoiding complacency: *the silent killer.* Keeping it a conversation, not a confrontation. Creating synergy by increasing morale. Appreciating the speed you are traveling relative to those around you. Stopping the *blame train.* Understanding the energy you give others. Approaching others: if you see something, say something, do something.

We fighter pilots are warned against the tendency to cut corners or to give a half-assed effort from the earliest days of our training. After losing my brother in an aviation accident, I was painfully reminded that no matter how good or skilled we might consider ourselves, if we become complacent in remaining fundamentally grounded in the basics of our craft, our craft will one day expose our weakness. Applying Band-Aids may cover problems temporarily, but relentlessly applying the fundamentals will cure problems permanently.

This book is about being a Target Leader on and off the job. Target Leaders inspire others to stay true to their core values and principles, no matter how tempting the easier road might be. Temptations to make the wrong choice knock constantly, yet the opportunity to make the right choice knocks only once. Target Leaders are not perfect, but they inspire the best decisions possible. They listen to understand, not argue. They are eager to hear valuable input that will make a process or environment safer, better, or more productive. They look inward for guidance, admit their mistakes, and take positive action to bring people together for the good of the organization. And what's good for the organization is great for its people.

In this book, we will reflect inward, admit mistakes, and adjust our attitude to become the mature Target Leader required to reach the next level personally and professionally. We will set expectations, monitor performance, learn to speak up, and have the courage to listen. We will communicate to understand before we make decisions. We will inspire others to go from the cellar to stellar. Along the way, I'll share some "gold nuggets," pearls of wisdom I've gathered through my experiences.

The Target Leader's attitude, temperament, disposition, and emotional intelligence will determine not only his or her altitude but also the altitude of those around him or her. Consider yourself like the sun, rising steadily and warming the rocks below. The resulting heat creates updrafts. Consider the people around you like eagles circling above the rocks and riding the updrafts from the heat you create. The more you heat the rocks, the higher they will climb.

High-performing organizations have employees who soar ever higher because of the energy created by the Target Leaders within the company. The effect is synergistic. Higher altitudes help us all see the bigger picture and gain perspective. We get a better vantage point and a larger margin of safety. New heights help us stay competitive and alert both personally and professionally.

As Target Leaders keep moving in the right direction, so moves the entire company. People are inspired to find new and exciting ways to motivate others to move with them, to work together safely in order to deliver the highest-quality products and services. Target Leaders have a fighter pilot's attitude to pursue perfection and achieve excellence. They will give their best effort this time with an eye toward improving next time.

Pursuing perfection does not mean you never make mistakes, but it does mean you are always improving. Achieving excellence means pushing the lesson learned forward, not pushing blame forward. It means pursuing *zero* harm to people and the environment and learning from our failures. Too many of our brothers and sisters have died at work or home doing a job we would consider routine, easy, or small.

This book is written for people like you and people like me: everyday people who work and live in a world that can be quite dangerous. I consider each of you fighter pilots. You are as highly skilled and as expertly trained in your craft as I am, yet mistakes, missteps, and mishaps still occur. I do not have all the answers, but I believe this book will lift you to a higher altitude. It will give you a better perspective on business, leadership, and life.

—✦—

Accuracy means something to me. It's vital to my sense of values. I've learned not to trust people who are inaccurate. Every aviator knows that if mechanics are inaccurate, aircraft crash. If pilots are inaccurate, they get lost—sometimes killed. In my profession life itself depends on accuracy.

—Charles A. Lindbergh,
The Spirit of St. Louis, 1953

—✦—

Because my life depends on accuracy, I need your help and your feedback. How can I be a better Target Leader? What lessons have you experienced that have inspired others to higher altitudes? I welcome your insights. By nurturing the Target Leader within us, we lift each other to greater heights. As this book raises your level of excellence, in turn, you will help raise mine.

ONE

LOSS OF A BROTHER

Many employees use the phrase "Be your brother's keeper" because it means something dear to each of us. It means we are a family. It means we watch out for each other like we would our blood brothers and sisters at home. We love each other. We care deeply for each other's health, safety, and well-being on and off the job, no matter what. Every now and then, we might bicker or fight among ourselves just like real siblings, but we work it out and move on. If anything tries to hurt us or come between us, we will bond together faster than a pack of hyenas chasing a gazelle wearing Milk-Bone underwear!

Within families, we give each other confidence; we help each other out when the pressure is on. We have the best of intentions for each other. However, a concoction of good intentions, a splash of overconfidence, and a twist of perceived pressure to hurry up can be a deadly mixture for any family trying to go somewhere or get something done. Unfortunately, my family and I have tasted this bitter witches' brew. I unintentionally failed to be my brother's keeper one particular afternoon.

Airplane pilots are nothing more than heavy-equipment operators, albeit fast-moving equipment. From an operator's standpoint, flying a jet is not much different from operating a crane, using a piece of factory equipment, working an oil platform, or driving a semi-trailer rig. Throughout the mid-1990s, I traveled up and down the East Coast while flying in air shows in a 1943 North American AT-6 "Texan," a single-engine aircraft that was used to train fighter pilots in World War II. The Texan is a popular plane and always a hit on the air show circuit. Many of these old war birds had nose art painted on the side of the fuselage or engine cowling, a tradition that started back in WWII. The plane I flew was named "the Howling Pig." I affectionately named her that because the big 600-horsepower Pratt and Whitney R-1340 radial engine drank gas like a pig as she howled her way through the sky. She was fully restored to her original form, looking just as she had when she first rolled off the assembly line. I kept her highly polished and in mint condition at all times.

AT-6 "Texan." Odie and John flying to an air show.

My right-hand man who helped me with logistics at these air shows and who also helped me keep the airplane in top condition was my older brother, John. We were 15 months apart in age. Growing up, we had our fair share of brotherly moments, both good and bad; we were always very close. Our parents divorced when we were young, so we depended on each other and on our mom for just about everything. However, after graduating from high school, my brother and I headed in two different directions. Once a diligent and hardworking student, John began taking the path of least resistance. Like our dad, he was a tremendous athlete and a talented football player, but he just couldn't seem to knuckle down when it came to doing schoolwork. To him college was not a place to study; it was a place to party. My brother handled all temptations with one word: "Yes!" Time and again, he would bite the inviting lure of temptation only to find himself in a mighty struggle to free his mouth from temptation's sharp hook of accountability.

My brother had several arrests for driving under the influence. He even totaled four vehicles. In one of the accidents, Johnny's best friend was thrown from the vehicle and was left paralyzed from the chest down. During this tumultuous period in his life, Johnny would set low goals for himself and then consistently fail to achieve them. His learning curve was completely flat. That is what alcohol addiction and drug use do; they take a serious toll on everyone involved. It's interesting to note that most bad things in life are easy to get into and hard to get out of. The addiction hook is sharp, strong, and difficult to dislodge. Tobacco, drugs, alcohol, gambling, and a myriad of other addictions have caught many unwary people. On the flip side, most good things in life are hard to achieve and easy to walk away from, such as going to college, studying hard, and landing the ultimate dream job.

Johnny banged his head against the walls of justice and accountability until one day he made a decision to change. With unwavering support from his family, especially Mom, John decided he was ready to enter rehab. He was 26 years old. The first step to change is deciding you're ready to change. It is not easy. Changing is hard work. Staying the same or quitting is easy. John decided he was ready to change, and change he did! Each day he spent in rehab, he matured by years. After nine years of Johnny's addiction, we were all very happy to have him back again. Now clean and sober, he reinvented himself. He became a licensed general contractor in Florida and began his career in the rebuilding efforts in Miami after Hurricane Andrew devastated so many communities in that area.

When he moved his business and young family to Atlanta near me, I enjoyed some of the best times with John, especially flying to air shows on the weekends with him. He was not a pilot, but he learned the air show business. He helped me set up the rides that we gave to the public, and he worked with the news media that promoted the air shows we went to. John was always very methodical in doing his part. I relied on him to have everything done just right, especially when it came to helping me prepare the Howling Pig for flight.

Many antique war birds, such as our AT-6, are powered by big, powerful radial engines, sometimes referred to as "round engines." For airplanes with round engines, the pilot should follow a particular procedure before starting the engine.

1. Parking brake—SET
2. Ignition switch—OFF
3. Rotate the propeller blades to check for evidence of hydraulic lock

You may have seen this in old World War II documentaries, where the airplane crew chiefs manually rotate or pull the engine propellers by hand before the pilot starts the engine. In the round-engine community, this procedure is known as "pulling the propeller blades through before start."

John pulling propeller blade through.

One of the problems that can occur in this process... This is a rare condition that occurs inside radial engin... past the lower piston rings or unburned fuel settles into... side of the bottom cylinders. The liquid may obstruct the ... that cylinder, and damage can occur as the engine is started ... ...owling Pig had nine cylinders, so the procedure was to pull the propeller blades through at least nine compression revolutions to check fully for hydraulic locks. If it took normal effort to physically rotate the propeller blades nine times, then you would know that the engine was clear to start. Unchecked internal engine damage may not be evident immediately. Engines have been known to fail even after becoming airborne.

Manually checking for hydraulic lock before engine start was my brother's job. One weekend, Johnny and I were wrapping up an air show in South Carolina. It was late on a Sunday afternoon. Rain showers and thunderstorms were common during that time of year, and that day was no different. As we were packing everything up, a massive thunderstorm loomed on the horizon, and it was coming our way. I was sitting in the cockpit and going through the preflight checklist while looking over my shoulder at the impending storm. Should we push the airplane into a hangar and wait out the storm? Should we hurry up and try to depart before the storm reached the airfield?

I could feel the pressure to leave mounting. My brother finished packing the plane. He appeared at the side of the engine and asked me whether the brakes were set and the ignition was off—standard procedure before he pulled the propeller blades through the required nine compression strokes.

As he reached for the propeller blade, my confidence in the engine's reliability mixed with my shortsighted good intent not to delay a second longer made me yell down to him, "Don't worry about it!" Johnny cocked his head to one side as if what I said made one side of his head weigh more than the other. Definitely a look that silently asked, "Are you sure?"

But before he could protest, I underscored my intention not to wait another moment by giving him a quick wave of my hand and stating, "The engine is fine! Let's get outta here!" With that, Johnny let go of the propeller blade, ran around to the rear cockpit, hopped in, and buckled up. As he was getting himself situated in the cockpit behind me, I'm sure he was thinking, "My brother's an expert. He knows what he's doing. I don't want him to think I don't trust his judgment by questioning him. Besides, we've never had a hydraulic lock problem before."

By now, the front edge of the storm was about two miles away. I completed the before-start checklist:

- Brakes—SET
- Fuel mixture—RICH
- Fuel primer—four strokes
- Throttle—OPEN one-quarter
- Ignition magnetos—BOTH
- Starter—ENGAGE

I pushed the starter button to the big R-1340, 600-horsepower radial engine. Care to guess what happened? The engine started right up, just as I predicted. As the motor belched white smoke from its massive exhaust stack, I called for taxi instructions and immediately received takeoff clearance. We blasted out of there before the storm hit, and we safely flew the entire way home to Atlanta without a problem. Even though nothing physically happened to the engine that day, something did happen. Johnny and I learned how easy it was to forgo a procedure and still get the job done.

The more we show others how to break the rules and still live, the easier it becomes for them to follow in our footsteps. After a while, we forget why the proper procedure is followed in the first place. The errant or unsafe method can become the norm, the way we do it around here. It's a deceptive trap set by everyone who either watched or participated in the shortcut and failed to correct it. Looking the other way sets a trap that may lay dormant for months, even years, until one day it springs its potentially lethal jaws on its unassuming victim(s)—SNAP! Now we are caught! Whether we wriggle free is all a matter of luck, reaction, and physics.

"There's been an accident."

Those of us in high-risk jobs and dangerous work environments such as aviation, utility, petroleum, chemical, construction, or manufacturing cannot rely on luck, reaction, or physics. We must rely on each other to do our jobs properly; otherwise, we might hear the dreaded words, "There's been an accident."

For my family, the date we heard that awful phrase was Friday, April 21, 1995, a mere six months after I had shown my brother that shortcut.

The Howling Pig was scheduled for an air show in Vero Beach, Florida, and it needed to be there Friday afternoon in order to fly the show that weekend. However, because of a previous scheduling conflict, I was not able to fly the airplane there myself. The plan was for Johnny to ride down with another pilot; I would take a commercial flight into Vero Beach later that night and join them. I would then fly the air show that Saturday and Sunday. Johnny arranged for a very qualified pilot, Craig Morrison, who also happened to be a good friend of ours, to fly the airplane for us.

Craig was a famous aviator in his own right, having been part of a well-known group of pilots called the Ravens that flew during the Vietnam conflict in Laos. Working as a Raven was an exhausting, high-risk, high-stress job. The casualty rate among these fighter pilots ran around 50% wounded and killed. Their planes were frequently hit by accurate and intense enemy fire. The Ravens developed excellent flight skills during their tenure flying in Laos, so I knew my brother was in good hands with Craig at the controls.

On Friday afternoon at around 4:30, Johnny and Craig took off in the Howling Pig and headed for Vero Beach. A few hours later, my phone rang. The voice on the other end said, "Jeff, there's been an accident."

"Wha-wha-what?!" I stammered.

"There was an engine failure," the voice explained. "The pilot was trying to glide the airplane down for an engine-out landing." This meant that the engine had failed in midflight.

"Were there survivors?" I asked.

"There were two fatalities," he said.

"Who was on board?" I asked, hoping against hope that it was not Johnny and Craig.

"We don't know who was on board," he said. "Everything burned on impact. We will need dental records to get a positive ID. We were hoping you could help."

How does one speak after hearing something like that? What could I possibly say? Despite my feelings of shock and disbelief, I heard myself say, "Our family dentist can get those for you." The whole time I was thinking about Mom, Dad, my brother's wife, and his two small children. I pulled out my wallet to look at the small picture I carried of Johnny's family. At that moment, everything became a blur. My eyes welled with tears as I touched the picture of his face. I knew Johnny was gone.

The following day, my parents and I were at the crash site, literally picking up the bits and pieces of Craig and Johnny that the coroner had failed to retrieve. I stood staring at the burned seat frame where my brother had been sitting. The airplane itself, once a beautiful machine that had flown the skies safely ever since it rolled off the assembly line in 1943, was sprawled on the sand in a burned and tangled mess.

Odie picking up the pieces.

THE ACCIDENT INVESTIGATION

Accident investigations are analogous to looking in the rearview mirror of our car. It's a small window to what is behind us. Certainly, much can be learned and gained by looking in the rearview mirror, but the real way to prevent accidents is by changing our view and looking ahead of the car, out the big window in front. Looking ahead means being proactive and seeing and avoiding accidents before they happen.

Unfortunately for me, in my rearview mirror was the National Transportation Safety Board (NTSB) pulling me over to investigate the crash. They are the investigative arm of the FAA. The NTSB spent several months methodically inspecting the shattered airframe and twisted engine to determine the cause of the crash.

After a thorough analysis of the wreckage, the lead NTSB investigator called me to discuss the findings. He said the Howling Pig's engine showed indications of hydraulic lock—exactly the kind of thing that can be detected and prevented by carefully pulling the propeller blades through before starting the engine. The entire bottom cylinder of the engine was blown off, which caused its total seizure.

Engine with bottom cylinder off.

Next came a few hard questions from the NTSB. These are the kinds of inquiries that I hope you never have to face if someone is hurt or killed on your watch at home or work. No doubt you will have to answer difficult investigative queries in a sensitive search to learn everything possible about what happened.

Because the Howling Pig's engine showed indications of hydraulic lock, the investigator probed, "Jeff, did your brother and the pilot know to pull the propeller blades through before engine start?"

Emphatically I said, "Yes, Sir, they knew to do that!"

I knew what his follow-up question would be. He asked, "Did they always follow the correct starting procedure?"

Hearing that question was like a punch in the gut. My mind immediately raced back six months prior when the thunderstorm was approaching the airport in South Carolina and Johnny was about to pull the propeller blade through and I yelled down from the cockpit, "Don't worry about it!" I remembered the quizzical look he gave me and my failure to properly respond to his questioning attitude. When I told Johnny, "The engine is fine! Let's go!" did I show him—he who trusted my judgment and experience as a pilot—that it was OK to break the rules if you felt the situation called for it?

After the investigator asked me that probing question, the silence on the telephone line between us told him the answer. I wanted to hide. I wanted to die. I thought I was a good pilot. I had flown hundreds of sorties as a mission-ready fighter pilot in the A-10 Thunderbolt. I was a commercial airline pilot. How could anyone die while flying airplanes on my watch, much less my brother? I wanted the investigator to know that Johnny and I were both committed to safety, were never complacent, and always followed procedures. We did not take shortcuts! Except for maybe that one time when we were in a hurry. But then again, that's all it takes—*one time*.

The painful conversation with the NTSB investigator continued. He said that he spoke to the fuel service tech, the person who fueled the Howling Pig before Craig and John departed that afternoon on its fateful flight. He was the last person to see them alive, and he witnessed their final preflight preparations and engine start. The investigator asked him whether he remembered seeing them pull the propeller blade through before they started the engine.

The investigator recorded what the fuel service tech recollected. "I don't remember them pulling the propeller blades through before they started the engine," he said, "but I do remember them being in a big hurry for me to finish fueling up their airplane because they were in a rush to get to some air show down in Florida."

Hearing him say that was a big blow to me. Did I show my brother something that negatively influenced his future work behavior? Did the shortcut I took encourage him to do the same? Did I demonstrate a technique that he mistakenly took as acceptable procedure? Was he pushing himself, or was I (the company) unknowingly pushing him to "hurry up"?

If we aren't willing to spend the time to do it right, then we had better be able to afford the price of doing it wrong. The bottom line is simply this:

it is better to spend a few seconds of your life doing it right than lose your life in a few seconds doing it wrong.

THE ROAD TO PERFECTION REQUIRES INWARD REFLECTION

Odie and his dad standing over the wreckage.

My mom took a picture of me standing next to my dad as we were looking over the wreckage of the Howling Pig. We are both staring at the burned-out seat frame where my brother drew his last breath. I had to stand there and reflect. Part of my healing was taking ownership, true ownership, of my previous work behavior with my brother in order for me to learn and grow from this. In these situations, being critical of the person in the mirror is the hardest thing to do, yet the road to pursuing perfection requires much inward reflection. It is vital to learning and growing as a person. Being honest with oneself is a healing ointment to a wounded heart, and it is most often the crucial first step to making positive changes going forward. I used to look at that picture of me standing at the wreckage next to my dad as a picture of failed leadership. But now, I consider it a failure only if I fail to learn and grow from the lessons. I consider it my duty to pass along the message to as many others as possible so they may learn and receive value from it.

On the occasion of every accident that befalls you,
remember to turn to yourself and inquire what power
you have for turning it to use.

—Epictetus, *The Enchiridion*, c. 125

MINING FOR GOLD NUGGETS

It takes tons and tons of gold-bearing dirt running through a sluice box to yield a few ounces of gold. Our brains are like sophisticated sluice boxes. As our lives progress, we pour in tons and tons of input and hope for a few flecks of golden wisdom. The tailings are nebulous nuggets of needless knowledge left over in our daily search for an ounce of valuable insight.

Finding nuggets of wisdom takes hours of work and time. It takes listening, reading, understanding, and communicating. Every so often, one big nugget of knowledge appears—a realization that truly makes a difference, an epiphany. Maybe it's the nugget of being able to learn from others that helps us see mistakes before making them again. Maybe it's an ounce of humility that helps us admit mistakes we don't want others to know about. Maybe it's sharing the wealth by being less arrogant. Maybe it's caring enough to pass our gold along so that others might profit from its value.

As a pilot, speaker, and consultant, I have been fortunate enough to gather a sizeable collection of gold nuggets and share them with families and corporate employees throughout my career. My goal is to pass as many of these gold nuggets on as I can and try to keep the nebulous nuggets of needless knowledge to a minimum.

Here is the first gold nugget I will pass along: How we behave and operate when no one is looking defines our character. Character is to the leader as culture is to the work group.

The sudden and tragic loss of my brother changed my life in profound ways. Just as excellent leadership begets excellence, poor leadership can yield poor results and tragic consequences. I remember telling a good air show buddy that there was no longer a "pot of gold" sitting at the end of my rainbow. A few weeks later he sent me a photograph with the caption,

"There IS a pot at the end of the rainbow." The photo showed a picture of a thunderstorm that had just passed over a large construction sight and left behind a huge rainbow. At the very end of the rainbow sat a Porta-Potty.

As I laughed at that bit of ironic humor, the picture made me realize that life rarely hands us a pot of gold, but when it does, we should cherish it. It can be lost in an instant, leaving what appears to be a pot of crap behind.

POSITIVE PERSPECTIVE

Putting things in positive perspective means seeing things in a different light. If you have ever complained about not having the right shoes to wear out for dinner, think of all the people who do not have shoes. If that is not enough perspective, then think of all the people who do not have feet. That's perspective. Some might always see a pot of crap at the end of their rainbow of life, but putting things into positive perspective means looking at life in a different way. Let's say your stomach is roiling because you have just eaten some bad sushi. While driving, you quickly do a time/speed/distance calculation to get home, and the math says, "You ain't gonna make it." Now, that Porta-Potty sitting at the end of the rainbow would be a wonderfully welcome pot of gold.

Life hands out many things we might consider crappy and unfair, but we can get bitter or we can get better. Which is it going to be? Chump or champ? Hero or zero? Cellar or stellar? Head up or head down? It's really up to us to choose. The choice as to how we look at things is not just a feeling; it's a decision we make each and every day. After my brother's accident, the phrase "your attitude determines your altitude" could not have been truer for me.

Adversity does not build one's character; adversity REVEALS one's character.

NEXT-LEVEL
LEADERSHIP:
TARGET LEADERS

Managers manage, and leaders influence. Not everyone is a manger, but everyone is a leader. This book is not about being a manger; it is about being a next-level leader—specifically, a Target Leader. We are all leaders. No matter how young or old we are, what our job title is, what level of management we are in, or how much or how little experience we have in a particular area, we all possess leadership ability to influence the behaviors, thought patterns, beliefs, and values of the people around us. Your leadership style might influence someone within the next minute, hour, or decade. Among your brothers and sisters, what is going to be your legacy as a leader going forward?

The day of my brother's accident, I was both manager and leader of that air show business. Even though I was not physically present on the dreadful day Johnny's accident unfolded, I had a leader's influence over his work behavior. I was a leader but not a Target Leader.

Leaders influence behaviors, but Target Leaders inspire behaviors. They inspire us to make positive choices and changes in life and leadership. Think of all the Target Leaders in your life who have really made a difference—maybe a parent, a teacher, a friend, a pastor, a complete stranger, or a coworker. I think of Target Leaders such as Mother Teresa, Gandhi, Nelson Mandela, and Martin Luther King Jr., who have influenced positive changes in the world. Target Leaders help us see the big picture, inspire us to believe in the future, and embolden us to make things happen. Bullies on the playground, racists on the street, and bigots in the office are all leaders. They influence people, but a Target Leader changes unscrupulous attitudes, faulty perceptions, and ignorant perspectives—and, ultimately, behaviors. The positive change that takes place adds value to all people. In the field, supervisors are leaders. If they decide to cut corners, take extended breaks, or pencil-whip paperwork, their behaviors will surely influence others to do the same. However, a Target Leader makes sure the *way it **is** done around here* is exactly *the way it **should** be done around here.*

> *A leader can light a fire under people's rear ends to get the work done. A Target Leader can light a fire in people's souls to get a lifetime's worth of work done.*

TARGET LEADERS INSPIRE

The first boss I ever had was a leader but not a Target Leader. He owned Phoenix Flight Signs, an aerial advertising banner–towing business that was located at the Grand Strand Airport in Myrtle Beach, South Carolina. It is now out of business, but when I was 19 years old, the company hired me as a banner tow pilot. I flew banners for it during college summer breaks.

The owner hired me because I was a good pilot with skill and I had great hand-eye coordination. After all, I had learned to fly when I was 14, soloed at 16, licensed on my seventeenth birthday, and acquired my commercial pilot's license when I was 18 years old. Getting a license to legally operate any type of machinery, such as driving a car or flying a plane, should be regarded as getting *a license to learn.* But at 18 years old, I didn't really understand that concept. I was confident in my flying skills, almost cocky, and I approached banner flying with the same self-assured poise.

Just because a pilot has the ability to fly an airplane well doesn't mean he or she has experience.

Unfortunately, being inexperienced meant I wasn't aware of all the things I needed to know to be a safe pilot. Nothing is more dangerous than an inexperienced equipment operator who thinks he or she has experience. It took me years to finally understand the phrase "You don't know what you don't know."

> *Experience is the window that allows us to see mistakes coming before we crash into them again.*

Flying advertising signs as a banner tow pilot up and down the coast of Myrtle Beach was a dream summer job for a college student. When the owner first hired me, I was overjoyed because the flying was fun and exciting. I paid close attention to everything I did because I did not want to mess anything up. However, as the weeks progressed, the newness wore off. The daily grind of flying turned into what can best be described as many hours of boredom punctuated by random moments of pure terror. Most of these terrifying moments were self-induced and served to remind me of how dangerous the job really was.

The owner wanted his employees to be productive. His mantra to his pilots was *fly, fly, fly!* Every morning as we did our preflight walk-around inspections, I remember his pacing back and forth, tapping his wristwatch, and saying, "Get 'em up! Get 'em up!" To him, time was money, and to that end he lit a fire under our butts to get the work done. As a leader, he definitely influenced my work behavior in all the wrong ways. Some of the flying we did was not always in the best interest of safety or our well-being.

The owner believed that safety happened automatically; therefore, so did I. My thinking was that he would not have hired me if he thought I was unsafe or couldn't fly the plane. Although I was inexperienced, I was skilled enough to physically operate the airplane well enough to fly banners. By hiring young pilots, the owner could save a lot of money on the payroll. Not only did we cost him less but also we followed his orders without question. Safety was something he neither emphasized nor rewarded. We flew planes with known maintenance issues but that were deemed by our boss to be safe. In hindsight it was anything but safe.

Unfortunately, his leadership style failed to account for our lack of experience, especially when it came to training us or having specific operating procedures in place. He did not teach us any sort of standards or routines. His "checkout program" basically was to see whether we had the ability and talent required to operate the airplane well enough to pick up and drop banners. As a new pilot, I worked diligently and managed to get through most of the summer incident free, until near the end.

Then I experienced a moment of terror that instantly reminded me how dangerous the job really was. The day started out like every other day: routine. It was a Saturday afternoon at the end of a seven-hour day of flying. I was flying back to the airport to pick up and fly the last banner of the day.

The airplane I was flying was an ex-military type known as an L-19 "Bird Dog," manufactured by Cessna. This was a distinctive and highly durable single-engine aircraft originally used by the U.S. Air Force as a forward observation plane during the Vietnam-era conflict. It was nicknamed the Bird Dog because the pilots flew it low to the ground to scout out, or bird-dog, enemy positions and then direct gunfire on those areas.

———

On 29 April 1975, the day before the fall of Saigon, South Vietnamese Air Force Major Buang-Ly loaded his wife and five children into a two-seat Cessna L19 Bird Dog and took off from Con Son Island. After evading enemy ground fire, Major Buang-Ly headed out to sea and spotted the aircraft carrier USS Midway (CV 41). With only an hour of fuel remaining, he dropped a note asking that the «runway» [sic] be cleared so he could land. Knowing there was no room for this to happen, Midway's commanding officer, Captain (later Rear Admiral) Lawrence Chambers ordered $10 million dollars worth of Vietnamese UH-1 Huey helicopters to be pushed overboard into the South China Sea. The Bird Dog that Major Buang-Ly landed with his family safely aboard Midway is now on display at the National Museum of Naval Aviation, Naval Air Station in Pensacola, Florida.

(Wikipedia, http://en.wikipedia.org/wiki/ Cessna_O-1_Bird_Dog)

———

In order to actually fly a banner, the pilot throws a grappling hook out the window of the airplane. The hook is attached to a 10-foot rope, and the rope itself is attached to a release at the tail of the plane. The hook dangles down behind the airplane at the end of the rope, and the pilot must fly low and fast toward a set of banner pickup poles. The banner is stretched out on the ground in front of the pickup poles, and there is a very long rope attached to it. The pilot flies the hook through the pickup poles, and the grappling hook snags the banner rope. The pilot has to time everything perfectly in order to hook the banner and safely keep flying while pulling something that is resisting being pulled.

On that particular day, I was flying the L-19 low and slow over the banner pickup area while trying to pinpoint the exact sign I was supposed to pick up. I had my head sticking out of the Bird Dog's window and was straining for a better view to find the correct set of pickup poles. The ground was completely cluttered with other banners that had already flown, so I was having difficulty figuring out which banner was mine. I'm 50 feet above the ground and flying along at 100 mph when all of a sudden, *the engine quit*! It didn't sputter or cough; it simply quit! One second, there was noise and the next, no noise. Nothing. The silence was deafening. For any pilot, this is definitely an underwear-changing event. My voice broke the silence with a choice phrase that started with the word "OH!"

I knew instantly why the engine had quit, but I could not dwell on that right then. I had to figure out how to get myself out of the stink I just stepped in. Nearly every emotion you can imagine—disbelief, fear, anxiety, and urgency—swept over me in one monster wave. Thank goodness I didn't panic. My right hand was on the control stick, and in one reactive motion, I pushed it forward to immediately establish a glide. This maneuver keeps the airspeed flowing over the wings. Airplanes technically don't need engines to fly; they need lift, and airspeed gives lift. The only way to maintain airspeed without an engine running is to head downhill. Pilots call this "trading altitude for airspeed." I had only 50 feet of that altitude to work with. My left hand was on the throttle, and I pushed it full forward, wide open—with no response from the engine. The engine had quit because I failed to properly manage the fuel between the left and right gas tanks. I ran the right tank completely out of gas.

In the blink of an eye, I reached up and switched the fuel selector from the empty right gas tank to the fuller left tank. I flipped the fuel boost pump switch to ON. I wished I had paid more attention to proper fuel management. I wished I had kept my altitude at least five mistakes higher. Now, I was hoping the engine would restart before I hit the ground.

Wishing is something you do when blowing out candles, throwing coins into a fountain, or pulling apart a wishbone. Hoping is something you do when waiting for rescue from a deserted island, a sinking ship, or a burning building. When it comes to flying airplanes, operating heavy equipment, driving a car, or working with dangerous machinery, wishing and hoping are neither the best nor the most reliable ways to safely get through the day. I was now relying on both to extricate myself from the mess I'd just gotten myself into.

Directly in front of the airplane was an open area of 5- to 10-foot-tall pine saplings. As the trees filled the front windscreen, I remember clearly thinking, "So this is what it looks like to die." I tried to soften the blow as best I could. I needed to "time the flare perfectly," which is pilot talk for pulling back on the control stick to level an airplane for landing, just as US Air Captain "Sully" Sullenberger did when he landed his "engine out" Airbus in the Hudson River and saved all on board. As the trees enveloped the windscreen, I pulled back on the control stick to lessen the impact.

Temporal distortion took over. This is an interesting phenomenon that occurs under extreme stress or during life-threatening events. Temporal distortion causes the brain to shift time and slows things down. Your brain is able to process intricate details in slow motion. A good friend of mine once reported his temporal distortion experience when he was involved in a midair collision between his F-16 fighter and a C-130, a large military transport airplane. As he was approaching the airfield to land, they collided. The collision ripped the F-16's nose cone completely away. Once it had been sheared off, my friend who was flying the F-16 said he remembered looking down and seeing the ground rushing by between his legs. He pulled the ejection seat handles. BOOM! The rocket under his seat fired instantly, but he remembers clearly reading individual instrument panel gauges as the ejection seat blew him out of the cockpit in less than a second.

I experienced the same phenomenon that day in the pines. My brain seemed to slow the passage of time. I remember seeing the trees enveloping the windscreen and then timing the gentle but aggressive pullback on the control stick to ease the impact. The next few seconds were surreal as the airplane dropped through the trees and hit the ground hard. The airplane shot back up in the air because just as it bounced, the fuel from the left tank reached the engine and it instantly came to life. VaROOM! The throttle was still wide open, and the abrupt burst of full power coupled with the initial bounce from hitting the ground had me 50 feet back in the air before I realized what had happened. This was another underwear-changing event. This time, the "OH!" was drowned out by the howl of the engine. My airspeed was dangerously slow, close to a stall—barely enough to create the lift required to sustain flight.

With the engine now running wide open and the airplane barely flying, I remember thinking I had a chance at landing in an open clearing just ahead. My only thought then was "Fight!" I needed to fight to keep the airplane flying at all costs. I finessed the control stick gently to keep precious airspeed and stay aloft.

"Stay out of the trees. Focus! Keep it flying. Keep it straight," I thought. The airplane labored toward the open field, and the momentum was enough to get me there. I landed safely!

The sound of the engine abruptly quitting and then restarting was enough to alert the ground crew that something was wrong. They turned to look in my direction, and in stunned amazement they watched the entire event unfold. I remember the foreman, Dennis, running to me as I sat in the cockpit. His eyes were as wide as saucers as he gasped, "What happened?"

Looking back, I wished I had the wit to say, "I don't know what happened. I just got here myself!" But all I could manage was a sheepish, "I ran the right tank outta gas." Dennis patted the side of the olive drab green–colored airplane I was still sitting in and quipped, "Well, you looked like a great big green bullfrog leaping in and out of those pine trees." So there I sat, a big green bullfrog who couldn't get out of the cockpit because the seat cushion was still clenched tightly between my buttcheeks. I knew I was a good pilot, but I surely didn't feel like one that day.

I was lucky, really lucky, to have survived that underwear-changing ordeal. But having to tell my boss that I had damaged his airplane and finding a clean pair of underpants on short notice weren't all that came out of the incident. I realized that I needed to create and follow a set of standards and checklists for each phase of the banner-towing day; otherwise, my workdays would be bound for the NFL—which means *not for long*.

My boss grounded me. He was not happy with my poor fuel management, but that's not why he enacted the punishment. No other airplane was available for me to fly until we fixed the one I trashed. Luckily for me, the damage was minimal. A few antennae were shaved off the bottom of the plane, and the propeller had a few nicks from the saplings. The mechanics fixed everything, and I was back in the air again within a few days.

As the summer wound down in Myrtle Beach, I convinced the owner to let me fly the Bird Dog back to Athens, Georgia, where I was going to college. I proposed that I could sell advertising signs to local businesses in Athens and fly the banners over the University of Georgia football games during the fall semester. He agreed.

I got the best seat in the house not only at all the Georgia games but also over Georgia Tech and Clemson games. I expanded my flying over Atlanta Falcons and Braves games, the Atlanta Motor Speedway, and Talladega. Thanks to the checklist I created and the procedures that I made myself follow, I flew safely over hundreds of outdoor venues, as well as three more summers at Myrtle Beach, without incident—until my last summer flying.

THREE

CHANGING OUR PERCEPTIONS

Target Leaders inspire better choices and help change our perceptions when needed. What we perceive is what we believe. What we believe gets our attention, focus, and commitment. What gets our commitment gets accomplished. What gets accomplished is what others see. What others see getting completed is what they believe. What they believe will then influence how they react and respond to what is around them. How a group behaves and responds creates the culture of how things get done.

With every sporting venue I safely flew banners over and with each passing summer I flew banners without incident at Myrtle Beach, my experience and my confidence grew. Even though the company, Phoenix Flight Signs, continued to experience numerous incidents and accidents each summer, none happened to me. My perceptions about the job began to slowly change. I knew flying banners was dangerous, but the longer I went without incident, the more I began believing that *bad things happen only to the other person, not to me.*

The day that my perception changed started like all the other days: routine. Five of us were flying banners that day when a massive thunderstorm was approaching the beach. I radioed back to the airport and told the owner that it looked bad and I was coming back to land. The other pilots agreed, but our boss insisted that we "keep 'em up, keep 'em up!" He told us the thunderstorm would pass well south of our location.

The bad weather moving our way was a group of severe thunderstorms known as a squall line. One minute I was flying on a bright, sunny day and the next I was tossed into the rinse cycle of the world's largest outdoor washing machine. The airplane was being buffeted by incredibly violent winds and rain that were pushing me out to sea. I tried to fly inland and land at a remote grass airstrip, but the weather had already reached that area, so I had to turn around. As I flew back to the beach, the storm completely overwhelmed me with its sheer power.

I released my banner and spotted a space to land in among the sand dunes—the only spot to land. Once again, I found myself wishing and hoping. I wished I had stopped the work and landed when I first saw the storm approaching. Instead, I now hoped to land safely in the sand dunes. The wind tossed the airplane around like a piece of tissue paper, and the rain was coming sideways.

> *It is better to be on the ground and wishing you were up in the air than it is to be up in the air and wishing you were on the ground.*

I did not know how the airplane would handle once it touched down in the rippling wet sand. I expected the worse—a crash that erupted in fire. To lessen the chance of fire after landing on an unknown surface, I decided to shut everything off just before touchdown. As I approached the sand dunes, I mentally prepared myself to execute the proper procedure:

- Throttle—IDLE
- Fuel mixture—CUT OFF
- Magnetos—both OFF
- Fuel selector—OFF
- Master battery—OFF
- Prayer—SEND
- Fingers—CROSSED

Gliding down, I landed the airplane in extremely soft sand. The airplane rapidly decelerated just as the two main wheels mired deep into the wet sand. The next sensations I felt were the lap belt and shoulder harnesses holding tightly against my upper body as I was pushed hard toward the windscreen and instrument panel. Not good! The Bird Dog is a "tail-wheel"-type airplane, as opposed to having conventional "tricycle" landing gear. Tail-wheel airplanes do not have a wheel directly underneath the nose; instead, they have a small wheel underneath the tail. The two main wheels got stuck in the sand, which caused the L-19 to roll up on its nose and then flip over on its back, leaving me hanging upside down by my seat belt and shoulder harness.

Unbelievable, I thought, as I hung in my seat. The only way out was to open the five-point quick-release harness lever. It worked as advertised because it quickly released me on my head—THUMP! I scrambled out and stood next to the plane. As the storm moved through, a crowd soon gathered around both me and the airplane. A woman asked whether I was OK. I replied that I was, and then she offered me a sandwich. That's how it is in the South. Anytime there is a gathering of people, somebody is going to get offered something to eat.

After that landing on the beach, I knew that my luck at surviving airplane crashes would eventually run out. I was the pilot in command (PIC). As much as I wanted to blame the owner for that mishap, I was the one responsible for my actions when operating a piece of equipment. I was ultimately accountable for my decision to keep flying and not land. My boss telling me to "stay airborne" was not an acceptable excuse to the

Stopping the work is always an option.

Federal Aviation Administration (FAA) for why I landed on the beach in a thunderstorm. That is like going to court for having an accident while speeding and telling the judge, "My boss told me to hurry." That would not go over well.

Fortunately for me, the FAA took no administrative action against me that day, but the beach landing was recorded and put in my official record. The airplane was a total loss. The owner lost a valuable piece of revenue-generating equipment, not to mention a great airplane.

I learned my lesson, and it completely changed my perceptions about my surroundings.

Unfortunately, the owner of Phoenix Flight Signs failed to learn from this. The following summer he lost another airplane under similar circumstances; however, the pilot was unable to safely reach the beach. The thunderstorm overwhelmed him just as it had me, and he was forced to ditch in the ocean. This from the NTSB report:

> *THE PILOT WAS ASKED IF HE WAS FAMILIAR WITH THE THUNDERSTORM AVOIDANCE PROCEDURES RECOMMENDED IN THE AIRMAN'S INFORMATION MANUAL. THE PILOT REPLIED THAT HE WAS AWARE OF THEM, BUT THAT HE COULDN'T SHUT DOWN BANNER TOWING OPERATIONS JUST BECAUSE A THUNDERSTORM WAS WITHIN 10 MILES OF HIS OPERATIONS AREA.*
> (http://aircrashed.com/cause/cATL87LA175.shtml)

Pilots who flew for Phoenix Flight Signs continued to fall victim to their inexperience and lack of proper training, as well as the owner's emphasis on productivity over safe work behaviors. Shortly after I left the company, a young pilot lost his life when his engine malfunctioned as a result of poor maintenance. He was attempting to land in the water but not too close to the surf where the people were swimming. The impact of hitting the water knocked him unconscious, and he drowned before the lifeguards could reach him. In the wake of this tragedy, the company ultimately went out of business. Unlike its mythological namesake, Phoenix Flight Signs never rose again from its ashes.

Experience is inevitable.
Learning is optional.

Although my boss had tons of experience, he failed to change his perceptions of how dangerous the work actually was for us. He operated his company the same way he flew airplanes: by the seat of his pants.

—⦿⦿⦿—

I did everything by the seat of my pants.
That's why I got hurt so much.

—Evel Knievel

—⦿⦿⦿—

Looking in our rearview mirror, perhaps we all can learn from these failures so that we can proceed forward in a safer manner. Maybe these shortcomings will help us change our perceptions about who we are, our ability to do things, and how we operate in a high-risk and dangerous work environment.

Changing perceptions means seeing what others are not seeing. When WWII bombers would return from dangerous missions, the mechanics repaired all the flak damage and bullet holes. When deciding where to put extra armor and metal plating for protection, engineers asked the mechanics, "Where are the areas on the plane that you have never patched holes?" Why would engineers want to protect areas that mechanics had never patched up before? Because those are the vital areas that have been hit, and the airplanes had never returned home to be patched. This different way of thinking ultimately saved countless lives.

Saving lives and making our surroundings better means thinking about ourselves as leaders in a different light. As leaders in our jobs, to our children, and to our friends, we have the ability to influence the behaviors of those around us, good or bad. Like the engineers of WWII, we should see ourselves as having the capability to profoundly affect people's lives both on and off the job.It means changing how we perceive ourselves. It means appreciating the size of the shadow we cast in others' eyes. Our behaviors are an outward manifestation of who we are and what we are about. They ultimately define our environment, our culture, our way of life.

I failed to appreciate the shadow I cast in my brother's eyes when I took that one shortcut with him. I was being a leader that day, but not a Target Leader. We need to be Target Leaders who pursue the positives and negate the negatives. Where needed, Target Leaders change perceptions in character and judgment. They inspire us to stand taller and to take more pride in ourselves and in our work. Their actions are grounded in principles, morals, and ethics. Being a Target Leader requires having a conscience and a valued commitment. It takes courage, fortitude, and grit to challenge apathy, complacency, greed, disservice, and difficulty. A Target Leader understands the inherent difficulty in flying against the headwinds of unspoken norms and tribal knowledge. Placing armor in the correct areas means protecting ourselves against the flak of mediocrity and the bullet holes of "the way we always do it around here."

You and I can take three paths to get things done:

1. Your way.
2. My way.
3. The BEST way.

Some leaders will take whichever path is convenient or easiest or offers the least resistance. Target Leaders look at what needs to be done and then pursue the best way to get there. Not his way, or her way, or my way—they encourage the BEST way. They change perceptions when needed in order to stay on the correct path. Just as importantly, Target Leaders know that plans change. Pride is set aside to help everyone remain flexible and adapt to the friction of change. Although the conditions of the work may change, the results should not.

High-performance organizations are constantly trying to identify who their Target Leaders are in order to help make a difference and inspire others to consistently choose the best way. I have heard Target Leaders referred to by many different names: real guys, trailblazers, front-runners, front-line supervisors, Mom/Dad, crew leaders, lead linemen, field reps, etc. Whatever their official title, you know who they are. You want them working for you. You want them to coach, mentor, and train others. You want them to lead the high-value jobs because when it comes to inspiring others, they are where the rubber meets the road.

As an observer of human behavior, I have noticed the following to be true. High-performing organizations actively promote and support Target Leaders who are exceptional at:

> *Being terrible at something is actually the first step at being good at something; unless you quit.*

1. emulating the organization's values and beliefs to make safety and operational excellence the overriding priorities among the employees.
2. maintaining a balanced and healthy working relationship between the company and the employees doing the work.

The by-product of these two items yields work behaviors from employees that ultimately define the organization's culture. Target Leaders establish and maintain the culture of the operation's environment, and the workers will operate within the norms of that culture.

As a Target Leader, creating and maintaining a balanced and healthy working relationship with your employees means figuring out when to manage and when to lead. Having that balance means being perceived by your employees as competent, forthright, and not afraid to say "I don't know." It means being approachable, nonjudgmental, even tempered, and personable and, most important, having integrity.

Nothing will change perceptions in others more quickly than a lapse in personal or operational integrity.

Maintaining integrity means not only being consistent in searching out the best way of doing things but also understanding the perceptions and beliefs of those on the team. The perceptions others have of themselves, of others, and of their surroundings will directly drive their actions, responses, and reactions within that environment. When people's perceptions do not accurately reflect reality, poor behaviors can happen, and unfortunate results will occur, such as my brother's accident.

Success is a habit, not a part-time job. Repeated slips will eventually turn into a permanent fall.

My perception that the engine on the Howling Pig would always function properly influenced my work behavior so that I didn't consistently follow proper starting procedure. And when the engine started properly and ran well, it gave a false positive to my brother. Six months later, my brother most likely repeated the same slipup. The outcome for him was a permanent and fatal fall. Once again, I was being a leader, not a Target Leader. I did the work my way, not the best way. This led my brother to do the work his way, not the best way, and he paid the ultimate price. Had we both seen ourselves in a different light, as Target Leaders, it would have changed our perceptions about the work, and my brother might be alive today.

After my brother's accident, I found myself looking back in life's rearview mirror at my banner tow boss. I reflected on his perceptions of us, his equipment, and how things should operate. He believed we were skilled enough to get the work done no matter the weather or circumstances. Many nonfatal slips occurred, until one resulted in a permanent fall. Had he changed his leadership perceptions, the reality would have been better training for us, higher expectations, and more oversight. In turn, he might still be in business today, and a young pilot might still be with us.

—◈◈◈—

Every accident, no matter how minor,
is a failure of the organization.

—Jerome Lederer,
director of the Flight Safety Foundation
for 20 years and NASA's first director
of manned space flight safety, 1991

—◈◈◈—

In our daily lives, if we perceive that we are better drivers than everyone else on the road, our behaviors will reflect that belief. We will multitask, drive too fast for conditions, daydream, put on makeup, shave, or read the paper during our daily commute. Many of us need to change the perceptions we have of our true driving ability. When workers perceive their technique as better than the approved method, they begin "technique blending" their way through the day, until one day their techniques meet reality.

When teenagers perceive that they know everything, arguments with parents are the behavioral result. My advice for these teens: "QUICK! Leave home while you still know everything. Come back when reality sets in." It won't take long to find out that life is like a tea bag: you don't know how strong or bitter it is until you sit in hot water awhile.

Parents and Target Leaders alike must keep one finger on the pulse of perceptions and the other on the pulse of reality. The idea is to be sure that the hearts of both entities are beating in sync so that behaviors respond to and reflect what is true, valued, and correct. Unfortunately, changing people's faulty beliefs or perceptions is quite difficult, especially if they have been operating in FD&H (fat, dumb, and happy) mode for extended periods of time. Perhaps you live or work with such a person. However, if you are a person that believes everyone else has a problem but you, perhaps you should reflect inward on the problem.

Target Leaders are experts in what is called MBWA (management by walking around). They get out from behind their desks and walk the floor, visit the job site, and connect with the people getting it done. Boots on the ground will always beat boots under the desk for effective guidance, increased morale, and optimal perceptions.

Get out there and put your eyeballs on the problem before it becomes a problem.

When addressing issues, some of the largest strides that companies have made in addressing problems are made before they become problems. When chief pilots of the airline get out from behind their desks and go ride the cockpit jump seats around the system, they are able to see reality, what's going on out there. They make sure the line pilot employee's perceptions of "the airline's system" are congruent with company values and beliefs. Rumors, mixed messages, unspoken norms, and ambiguities are cleared up. Misperceptions get realigned with reality.

A senior environmental health and safety manager at a petroleum company told me that the greatest improvements his company made in safety on the job came when company management gave Target Leaders the time to be more visible and accessible to the line employees working in the field. He said it was a "step change" when it came to lowering their overall total recordable incident rate (TRIR).

He mentioned that the visits were most effective when they came at different times and during all shifts, not every Monday at 9 a.m. They set up a schedule where, over time, they touched every single shift and visited every region. For some of the leadership, covering all the areas took a few weeks, but this was a critical procedure. By getting to know the people doing the work, who they were, and what they did, the leadership kept a finger directly on their pulse of perceptions. By understanding each shift's strengths and weaknesses, the Target Leaders made sure the pulse of the company's expectations was being transmitted and aligned with employee reality in the field. Where they found misalignment, the Target Leaders were responsible for figuring out how to modify their perceptions to come back into alignment with corporate reality.

Chemical plants, factories, mills, construction sites, oil rigs, petroleum plants, utility line crews, power plants, aviation, and medical practices are all inherently dangerous places to work. It's only when we change our perceptions and appreciate the danger, learn the equipment, follow checklists, peer check, and adhere to established safety protocols that we are able to manage the risk of working in such environments. The better we are at managing these risks and driving employee vigilance, the safer our surroundings are for everyone.

> *You make a living by what you get. You make a life by what you give.*

Believe You Me

Believe you me, if I think my surroundings are dangerous, I pay attention. I will maintain a greater sense of awareness of what is around me. I will take more precautions. I'll make sure no one in the family is wearing Milk-Bone underwear if we go on a safari. I will work slowly, conscientiously, and carefully if I believe I can get hurt. Others around me will see my commitment because my work behavior will reflect what I believe.

If I believe driving a car is always dangerous, then I will commit my actions behind the wheel to reflect that belief. I will slow down a bit more. I'll think twice before I attempt to multitask and drive or opt not to wear a seat belt. When cell phones first came out, I loved the idea of being able to drive and schedule appointments, text, and talk to clients. No laws were yet in place to hold drivers accountable if they caused an accident while using these new communication-distraction-interruption devices. Isn't it interesting

> *Be accountable, not held accountable. There is a difference.*

that when we fail to hold ourselves accountable, society must enact laws and regulations to do so?

Going with the flow of the people on the road, I, too, believed in my personal experience and ability to drive the car safely while multitasking with my cell phone. However, when my daughter turned 16 and got her driver's license, I knew the "self-preservation and awareness" chip in her brain did not have near the data that mine had. So, I gave her some very clear directives before handing over the keys to my beloved truck: "No texting or talking on your cell phone while driving. Understood?"

Looking me straight in the eyeballs, she enthusiastically answered, "Yessir, Daddy!"

Believe you me . . .

- She clearly got the message!
- She would comply with my crystal clear directive.

Two weeks later, she pulled in the driveway with a rash. Only the rash was not on her skin—it was on my truck. Diagnosis: Cell Phone Rash

Prescription: Rant for 10 minutes and then remove all driving privileges until further notice.

Believe you me, I was not happy with my daughter!

Truck cell phone rash.

As I was administering the 10-minute-rant dosage, my daughter interrupted me with, "Yeah, but you do it." Undeterred, I continued with the rant, "Yeah, but I have more experience, knowledge, and skill driving than you; besides, it's *my truck*, I'm the parent, and you do as I say, not as I do."

Now, how is that working for me? As I'm staring at the dent on my truck bumper, my conflicted soul takes me backward in time to reflect on a few pictures hanging in the gallery of my mind's eye. A voice quietly whispered, "Do you believe the rant is the cure?"

It was the voice of my brother, taking me back to his accident. I suddenly felt extremely grateful that I was looking at my truck bumper with a dent on it instead of a body bag with my daughter in it. As her parent, I influenced her behavior, but as her dad, I failed to inspire her behavior. I was being a leader to her, but not a Target Leader.

Remember—leaders influence; Target Leaders inspire. What will be your legacy?

As Target Leaders, we are on duty 24-7 inspiring those around us to pursue perfection and achieve excellence. Being a Target Leader is not easy. It takes managing many different aspects of work and family life. It means staying tuned into what you believe and recognizing how your beliefs turn into actions for others to see. Just because things may work out well for you does not mean that those same things will work out well for others.

The absence of an accident does not necessarily indicate the presence of safety.

The reality is that danger lurks around every corner: it is present on every job site; it rides along with us in every vehicle; it lives in each of our homes; it follows us down every step in a stairwell; it walks with us on every sidewalk. Danger flies on every airplane and sails on every cruise ship. Danger is in every schoolyard and down every dark alley. Danger is all around us. It never goes away.

The good news is this: we will be safe from danger as long as we properly manage or mitigate the risks associated with living in an innately dangerous and hazardous environment. To that end, *believe you me . . .* all accidents associated with our surroundings are preventable. Many of you just did a reader's "stutter step" after reading that statement. In chapter 15, "Picture Your Perfect," I will explain why it is important for Target Leaders to set an expectation that all accidents are preventable.

In discussing with senior leadership at a major automobile manufacturing company the concept of our surroundings always being dangerous, I was getting some push back on the semantics of it all. One man did not want me telling the employees they worked at a "dangerous facility," or their job was hazardous, or their "surroundings at work were always dangerous." He asked me, "Odie, do you consider your job flying as an international airline pilot as always being dangerous?"

Without hesitating, I said, "Absolutely! As a matter of fact, the modern, state-of-the-art Boeing 777 airliner I fly today is just as dangerous as the airplanes that flew back in the 1930s!"

He looked at me incredulously and said, "You're kidding me! You mean to tell me that the modern jets flying today are just as dangerous as the airplanes the Wright Brothers flew?"

With a grin I said, "Yes, the dangers are exactly the same, with one exception. The airplanes that flew back then flew sooooo slowly that when they hit the ground, the passengers just barely died."

Everyone laughed as I got my point across. The dangers employees face in modern business today are exactly the same as when their business first began because the result of one mistake is exactly the same: injury or death. If pilots, operators, shift leaders, janitors, plumbers, welders, doctors, nurses, and others believe their work is inherently dangerous, they will strive to mitigate the risks associated with the danger.

—⟨⟩⟨⟩⟨⟩—

I thought her unsinkable and I based my opinion on the best expert advice available. I do not understand it.

—Philip A. S. Franklin,
vice president of the White Star Line, sobbing to
reporters the day after the Titanic sank, April 15, 1912

—⟨⟩⟨⟩⟨⟩—

The *Titanic* was deemed "unsinkable" by the operators (captain and crew) and by the company. Danger was put in the company closet along with the extra lifeboats that should have been on board. The faulty belief triggered many unsafe and high-risk behaviors, and now the word "Titanic" lives in infamy. Sadly, we are only as good as our last accident. Too often, the further we distance ourselves from our last "oops," the more likely we are to become complacent and repeat it.

Our second "Titanic" came with the sinking of the state-of-the-art cruise ship *Costa Concordia* off the coast of Italy in January 2012. The world was instantly reminded of how dangerous operating a ship really is. Unfortunately, it takes a major accident to refocus our beliefs about the reality of our work and to underscore the importance of following approved processes and procedures.

DANGEROUS VERSUS SAFE

By embracing the belief that our surroundings are dangerous, in our actions we will do what is necessary and required to make our surroundings safe. We stay safe from danger by being diligent in applying the human error-prevention tools, processes, techniques, and procedures that our company puts in place in order for us to get the job done safely. If pilots or ship captains have the attitude and mind-set that behind every journey lurks danger, their vigilance will remain heightened. Their willingness to slow down and proceed with a bit more caution would be widely accepted by every person associated with the job.

I was speaking at an all-employee safety leadership conference when afterward one of the field supervisors approached me and said, "Odie, you just changed what I believe about my work environment. The work I do is always dangerous, but it's up to me to be sure I work safely." I told him that I could not have said it any better!

When trying to avoid danger completely, I've heard many companies tell their employees that they should never take a risk, but I don't think that's exactly what they mean. If we took that suggestion literally, we would never go anywhere, get any work done, drive a car, play baseball, cook dinner, mow the lawn, use a paring knife, walk down a sidewalk, talk to a stranger, climb a tree, or have children.

In order to live our lives, we take educated and calculated risks in nearly everything we do. Subconsciously, we have an internal matrix of risk versus reward that we evaluate before we act. The better we are at minimizing the risks, the safer we will be. But the higher the reward, the higher the risk many of us are willing to take. This is known as "risk tolerance." Some of us have a higher tolerance for risk in order to achieve a certain reward.

Our risk tolerance starts as soon as we roll out of bed in the morning and our feet hit the floor. We begin to automatically manage the risks and rewards of our behaviors and actions. For example, what is your risk tolerance for eating a big cream-filled donut with chocolate sprinkles for breakfast every morning? It has a lot of delicious rewards, but we must weigh (literally) the risk of that continuous behavior. The reward is the delicious taste, but the risk of eating too many tasty treats is that eventually our shadow is going to weigh about 50 pounds, and if we went hiking in the mountains, Bigfoot would take *our* picture.

We must constantly evaluate the risk we are willing to take to achieve a certain reward. Our tolerance for risk and how we analyze our surroundings change over the course of our lives. Age, experience, and skill play a big part in our tolerance for risk versus reward.

As experienced adults, we shake our heads ruefully at the incredible risks some of our teenagers are willing to take in order to reap what we would consider to be of little or no reward. Think of how many accidents have happened because the operator or the company was willing to tolerate a bit more risk than what was acceptable or wise. Think of the oil spills, sinking ships, refinery explosions, aviation crashes, or building collapses that have occurred because the risk tolerance among those collective corporate officers grew too high.

Cruise ships operate in much the same manner as commercial airliners. The company outlines approved procedures and routes that we are expected to follow in order to deliver our passengers safely to each destination. Through satellite GPS tracking data, company leadership can clearly see the actual course their airplanes or ships are taking. When they see their passenger vessels consistently taking a course other than what is approved, then believe you me, a course correction must be implemented—and quickly!

When silence meets truant behavior the word spreads.

If leadership does not step in and give corrective action at the first sign of trouble, the bad behaviors will continue. They do not heal themselves and get better with time.

When the *Costa Concordia* ran aground off the coast of Italy because it sailed too close to shore, numerous investigative reports indicated that "the dangerous maneuver was not an isolated incident. Residents [there] reported that such maritime greetings are commonplace." ("Cutting Close to Shore 'A Nice Tradition, Normalissima,'" Julia Stanek, Giglio Porto; http://www.spiegel.de/international/europe/cutting-close-to-shore-a-nice-tradition-normalissima-a-809580.html)

The article "Cutting Close to Shore" goes on to report that the mayor of Giglio, the island where the mishap occurred, wrote an e-mail to a friend and captain with the cruise ship company to thank him for passing close by the island, saying it was an "unequalled spectacle" and had become an "indispensable tradition."

According to residents of the island, the tradition had been going on for years, and everyone just hoped that nothing bad would ever happen. That hope failed for the people who lost their lives on *Concordia* that Friday night. According to the *Il Tirreno* newspaper, Antonello Tievoli, who was the restaurant manager on board the *Costa Concordia* and also a Giglio island native, called his parents that Friday afternoon and told them that he would be passing by their house on the island's west coast, saying, "We'll be coming at about 9:30 p.m.; look out the window."

This would be analogous to a commercial airliner establishing an "indispensable tradition" of flying low through the Colorado Rocky Mountains and a flight attendant calling her parents who live in a mountain house and telling them, "We'll be coming by at about 9:30 p.m.; look out the window."

Mix overconfidence and errant behavior with flying low and an "unequaled spectacle" is bound to result.

After unequaled spectacles happen, companies go into self-preservation mode. All too often, it's the operator(s) who are thrown under the bus first. Such was the case with the *Costa Concordia* captain. In the days following the sinking, the company told the world he was sailing on an "unapproved route." It did not take investigators or the rest of the world very long to figure out the rest of the story.

Let me say that I am not judging the company for its behavior or the captain for his. Systems are in place for judging, and they aren't me. I read the reports to learn, not judge. In my life, I can say that I have tolerated a bit too much risk for seemingly little reward. Figuratively speaking, think of how often you've sailed your life's ship too close to shore for a cheap thrill or to show off and got away with it. You rationalized in your mind, "Everyone else is doing it and getting away with it; why can't I? If the situation calls for it, what is the harm?"

Believe you me, that way of thinking has caused untold damage, destroyed equipment, and disrupted lives in corporations around the globe. That way of thinking is known as "situational compliance," which is nothing more than turning black-and-white rules gray if we feel the situation calls for it. As high-performing individuals, we cannot allow ourselves to decide in which situations we will follow the rules and in which situations we won't. If rules or policies need to be changed, proper channels and protocols are in place to formally do just that, and it is not done by us, on the fly in the field.

Reflecting inward, I fell victim to a bit of situational compliance that day with my brother. I felt the situation called for not pulling the propeller blade through because the storm was coming and I did not want to delay. Six months later, my brother fell victim to a bit of situational compliance because he, too, got in a hurry. He paid the ultimate price. All those ship captains who collectively sailed on the unapproved route fell victim to situational compliance until the one captain paid the ultimate price.

Be on guard for situational compliance. It most often rears its head when we are faced with:

- A change.
- A challenge.
- An opportunity.
- A dilemma.
- A pressure to "hurry up" and "get it done."

When any of these situations arise, Target Leaders inspire the correct responses and the right decisions from their people. *Believe you me*, how you and I respond to changes, challenges, opportunities, dilemmas, and pressures will influence others around us. As Target Leaders, our responsibility is to inspire others to make the right choice, no matter the situation.

THE BLAME GAME

Do you know people who are never wrong? Even when the evidence is clear they made a mistake, someone or something else is always to blame. I call it "playing the blame game." As a matter of fact, right after the first blame game was ever played, the fashion industry was born.

In my opinion we can trace the blame game, its participants, and how it got started back to the Garden of Eden. The players were one man, one woman, and one convincing serpent. The game started with one temptation, an apple.

A few bites later and the blame game was on. When Adam was caught with apple pulp stuck between his teeth, he pointed his finger directly at his wife and blamed her. Eve, being a fast learner of how to pass the buck of blame, quickly blamed the snake. The snake, not such a fast learner, has been crawling on its belly ever since. I only wish the snake were still walking upright—that way, I could see it coming ahead of time and I wouldn't act like a spastic fool when it slithers by.

Each participant finished the blame game that day by failing to accept responsibility for his or her actions. Being ushered out of the garden draped in fig leaves, the fashion industry was born. I'm sure Adam was heard muttering to his wife, "Lead me not into temptation, for I can find it myself."

Humankind has been playing the blame game ever since. Life's temptations beckon us constantly. The quicker we accept our choices as decisions when a temptation comes before us, the better chance we have not only to conquer the blame game ourselves but also to help others do the same. When we stuff ourselves with good food, we do not blame the cook for preparing such a good meal. We do not blame the pastry chef for making cream-filled donuts after we have eaten a dozen. We do not blame the wine maker for making such good Cabernet when we get *shi-fahzed* at Thanksgiving. These are choices we make.

> *The opportunity to make the right choice knocks once, but temptations to make wrong choices knock constantly.*

Unfortunately, temptations, bad choices, and the blame game that follows are played in nearly every business, home, and school. When wrong choices are made and breakdowns and failures result, the normal reaction is to put our finger in someone else's chest and blame him or her. Illustratively speaking, the Garden of Eden proves that it is in our DNA to cast blame and make excuses for our mistakes. We don't mean to do it; it's just the easy thing to do. We all experience a natural human tendency to want to protect ourselves from being embarrassed, looking stupid, appearing incompetent, or letting others down.

However, finding fault in others and pointing fingers outward both eventually create a culture of mistrust and dishonesty among honest people. Such acts create a divisive and caustic work culture. To get to the root of any failure, the people involved have to undertake a high degree of inward reflection. Failures are a part of life, and when they do happen, it is vital that we accept our part so that others will accept their part.

Millions of dogs in doggie heaven right now are reminiscing with each other about all the times they got blamed for the gas that was passed at the dinner table. They got tossed outside while the real culprits, Uncle Frank and Aunt Edna, were still inside crop-dusting their way around the dessert table.

Who breaks the culture of blame? Who is going to be tough enough, responsible enough, to stand up and say, "It was me"? Who is going to be the first in the group to throw himself or herself in harm's way and take the hit for the rest of the team? When the blame train begins rolling down the track and everyone is hopping on board, who is going to make the sacrifice and stop the train from rolling? Only one person can stop the blame train in its tracks, and that's the one who is in charge.

Target Leaders, you know who you are. The people who work with you, for you, and around you also know who you are. You are the ones at the top. You are the conductors who can stop any blame train from rolling and prevent it from derailing an entire group of well-intentioned passengers. Simply apply the brakes with your pointy finger by pressing the button labeled "STOP THE BLAME TRAIN." The button can be found in the middle of your chest. This will inspire others to do the same.

When people begin reflecting inward first, many issues and concerns will expose themselves that would otherwise go unseen and undiscovered. You will find the button in the middle of your chest hard to push at first. If it sticks, go find some WD-40 and give it a few squirts. Find people in your life who are like WD-40. They are the ones who can help you grease the skids, give you a boost, or support you when you've made a poor or unhealthy choice. This world is very forgiving of those of us who can fess up and take ownership of our mistakes.

> *If it's supposed to move but doesn't, use WD-40. If it's not supposed to move but does, use duct tape.*

Think of all the public figures who have committed some pretty egregious errors but when they admitted their part and took responsibility for their decisions, they won the blame game. It takes fortitude; it takes will power.

Air force pilot training did a great job of teaching us that making excuses for poor performance or blaming something or someone for our bad judgment would not be tolerated. Early on in training, I remember one of our pilot instructors debriefing a fellow student about how poorly he did that day making level turns. The instructor was pointing out the specifics of where the student was climbing 300 feet too high here and then losing 350 feet while turning there. The student interrupted with a "Yeah, but . . ."

In the English language, if you ever wonder the exact starting point where an excuse begins, it is right after the word "but." As soon as the student uttered the words "Yeah, but," the instructor knew an excuse was about to come forth. I looked up and saw an immediate shift in his facial muscles. His eyes grew so thin with anger he could have blindfolded them with dental floss.

> *The opportunity to squash excuses and eliminate blame knocks once, but the temptation to sidestep personal accountability knocks constantly.*

The instructor pilot's physical shift in demeanor went unnoticed by the student as he blurted out his excuse for not making level turns. This is what he told the instructor: "Yeah, but the reason I didn't make levels turns was because the clouds were sloping."

The next thing I heard was a small nuclear explosion from the instructor's mouth: "YOU MEAN TO TELL ME YOU CAN MAKE LEVEL TURNS ONLY IF THE CLOUDS ARE LEVEL?"

"Uh, well, uh, yeah, but . . ." stammered the student with the flat learning curve. By now the instructor was on his feet and leaning forward.

He continued, "DO YOU MEAN TO TELL ME THAT BEFORE YOU FLY, YOU'RE GOING TO CALL UP THE METEOROLOGIST AND ASK, 'HEY, ARE THE CLOUDS SLOPING, OR ARE THEY LEVEL TODAY'? WHAT IF THE FORECAST IS FOR LEVEL CLOUDS AND YOU GET AIRBORNE AND THE CLOUDS CHANGE? ARE YOU GOING TO TURN THE JET INTO THE GROUND IF THE CLOUDS ARE SLOPING INTO THE GROUND?"

"Uh, well, uh, no, Sir." And with that, there were no more excuses. No more blaming the clouds or anything else for shortcomings or errors. The student pilot I am referring to here was Michael Anderson, who, after graduating from pilot training, rose through the ranks at NASA to eventually become an astronaut. He was the payload commander aboard the space shuttle *Columbia*. Along with the rest of the world, I watched in dismay and disbelief as *Columbia* disintegrated before our eyes.

After the shuttle disaster, investigators determined a loose tile was what delivered the fatal blow. But just as fatal, investigators uncovered a pervasive culture at NASA wherein no one wanted to be blamed for decisions that might cause delays, cost more money, or impact the shuttle schedule. The investigative board also determined that many of the root cause errors were echoes of the *Challenger* accident.

Never underestimate how difficult it is to learn from previous mistakes.

I am not blaming NASA for Mike's loss by any means. Many reports and much analysis were published about what happened and how to prevent a tragedy like that from happening again. Lessons like these can translate directly not only to us as individuals but also to our organizations. Companies inadvertently create a culture of blame when leadership wants to know "who is at fault" after something goes wrong. When failures or breakdowns occur and leadership walks into a room full of people and begins pointing fingers, the room quickly turns into a room full of porcupines. Every person in there bristles up. They all look like porcupines as every finger in the house is sticking out. However, a company with Target Leadership wants to know, "How do we prevent this from happening again?" They look to repair the process, not replace the people.

It is easy to armchair quarterback a dead pilot or blame the operator for the decisions he or she made. Most of these problems are systemic, and the operator was simply operating within the norms of the system. However, systems are run by a collection of people, individuals. As an individual in the system, be responsible and be accountable for your part.

Where there is a will, there is a way. Where there is no will, there is an excuse.

WHAT A
DUMB ACT

Whn it comes to determining our last flight, fighter pilots know one of two things. Either we know it's our last flight or we do not know it's our last flight. The idea is to make sure retirement determines our last flight and not some dumb act. The same can be said of your "fighter pilots." The Department of Labor has a statistic that says 90% of accidents that happen are "behavior related." I guess that means 90% of the time, a reasonably smart person committed a dumb act that ultimately resulted in an accident. It is not my place to judge anyone's dumb act; after all, I have certainly committed my fair share of them. I see it as our duty and responsibility to learn from those who have gone before us. We should endeavor to glean whatever lesson(s) a dumb act has left behind.

After an accident, I have heard supervisors lament the stupidity of the person who committed the dumb act that ultimately caused the mishap. The reality is that high-performing organizations do not hire stupid people. Rarely do these types of people make it through the hiring process, even though every now and then one slips through. When you have absent minded human air exchangers working in your department, you basically have three options:

1. Fire them—quick!
2. Retrain and refocus their energy. Pair them with a mentor. Document everything. Monitor their performance.
3. Remove all warning labels and let the problem fix itself.

OK, I'm just kidding about the third option. The point is that organizations retain only the best and brightest workers—us! Even then, each of us has done some really stupid things that made others look at us and say, "What a dumb act!"

I remember making coffee in the galley of the airplane and greeting the passengers as they were boarding the flight to Barcelona, Spain. I opened the sugar packet and poured the sugar into the galley garbage and threw the empty sugar packet into my cup of coffee. The passengers who saw me do that stopped dead in their tracks. Their eyes grew as wide as saucers while they looked at me. Nobody said anything, but the facial expressions said everything: "What a dumb act! If that pilot doesn't know the difference between a coffee cup and a galley garbage, how is he going to know the difference between Barcelona and Bangkok?"

Near misses, incidents, and gaffs happen all the time to smart, highly trained, well-intentioned people. We are not dumb people. This begs the question, Why do smart people do dumb things? I consider myself able to pontificate upon such a question. Too many times I have found myself working a job and the next thing you know, I've done something really dumb. Sometimes I just roll my eyes at myself,

> *It is important that we learn from the mistakes of others because we won't live long enough to make all of them ourselves.*

and then sometimes it's a real attention getter. Smart people are supposed to use their superior skill, intellect, and judgment to avoid dumb situations where they must use their superior skill, intellect, and judgment to extricate themselves. Smart pilots fly the airplane with their head, not their hands. It's the same with any job.

Reduce the surprise time to eliminate dumb acts.

The equipment we are operating or the airplane we are flying may disappoint us when it fails to work properly, but equipment failures should never surprise us. Equipment operators do not like surprises, especially when lives are at stake. To eliminate or reduce surprise time, many of us are required to spend time in simulators in an effort to replicate everything that could possibly go wrong when operating the machinery. Thus, the surprise time to the operator in the real world is greatly reduced when something goes wrong or fails.

Airline pilots are required to go through what I call "dial-a-disaster" training. This is an annual event that is flown in a simulator. The simulator instructor can dial up any disaster, and the pilots must handle it safely and effectively. Engine failures, wind shears, cargo fires, flight control malfunctions, crazy passengers—you name it; we handle it. Crashing the simulator while handling emergencies is highly frowned upon and is regarded in the same manner as if the plane had crashed in the real world. BAD!

Simulator instructors are constantly looking for areas that need improvement. Their job is to identify weak areas that, if left unchecked, could potentially lead to future accidents. They are not looking to hammer the pilots; they are looking to hone the process. This facilitates better airmanship, procedures, and policies for all pilots.

I have worked with companies that have held employee workshops analogous to simulator training. They discuss all the areas that may surprise workers on the job. Then they debate how best to handle the situation(s) ahead of time so there are no surprises if the situation actually arises. This gives the team a backup plan of action. Thinking through the contingencies and "what ifs" helps the team rely on logic rather than luck to mitigate dumb acts associated with surprises.

—◈—

I'm a great believer in luck, and I find the harder I work, the more I have of it.

**—Thomas Jefferson, third president
of the United States (1743–1826)**

—◈—

Going through life, we carry two buckets: a luck bucket and an experience bucket. The result of every dumb act we commit relies on what we have in our luck bucket and what we have in our experience bucket. As we grow, we continually fill our experience bucket with values, skills, training, knowledge, and wisdom. However, our luck bucket is finite in capacity, and its content level is unpredictable. The trick is to make sure our luck bucket does not run out before our experience bucket fills up. We never know exactly when our luck will run out. Experience tells us that hoping for a bit more luck after getting ourselves into a tight situation is not the path to longevity.

d'oh (interjection): used to express recognition of a foolish blunder or an ironic turn of events (*Merriam-Webster Dictionary*); expressing frustration at the realization that things have turned out badly or not as planned (*Oxford English Dictionary*; first included in 2001).

"D'oh!" is not only Homer Simpson's catchphrase but also what a pilot says right after he or she accidentally lands with the landing gear up. After saying that, the next thing the pilot does is put the landing gear handle in the cockpit to the DOWN position. Unfortunately, the landing gear motor is not designed to raise the entire weight of the airplane off the runway after the pilot has accidentally bellied it in. "D'OH!"

I doubt that aircraft manufacturers will make the landing gear motors stronger, so the solution to fixing dumb acts like that lies with the human—in this case, the pilot. Timing rules the world. The proper timing for the gear lever to be placed in the DOWN position is before landing, not after. At your work as well as mine, I bet thousands of little things need to be done with proper timing. How do we keep track of properly timing all these critical little things that keep us from belly-landing in our job? Checklists!

Checklists are created to help us properly time who is going to do what and when it should be done. Checklists do not explain how the equipment operates; we get that with training and operation manuals. Checklists help us stay on track, keep us on pace, and provide an order of operation. Checklists also help prevent helmet fires. That's when your brain gets so overwhelmed by the situation you've created for yourself,

Using checklists will keep helmet fires at bay.

it catches on fire inside your helmet. Even though you may have run the checklist a thousand times and you know it by heart, the one time you fail to run it properly, or get distracted and fail to pick up sequentially where you left off, is the one time you may find yourself replacing your landing gear motor because it burned itself out trying to lift your airplane off the runway.

Companies work very hard to hire smart, careful people: skilled technicians, equipment operators, mechanics, welders, and the like. It is up to us to make sure *what we do* is exactly the same as *what we should do*. Many times, succumbing to the temptations to cut corners, slack off, or not comply with proper procedure can easily cause highly skilled, well-trained individuals to have accidents. Afterward, we reflect inward and wish that *what we did* was *what we should have done*. These dumb acts fall neatly into what I call doing something DDD: dumb, dangerous, or different.

> Dumb—Done without thinking things through logically; snap decision; knee-jerk reaction.
> Dangerous—Done without following proper processes, procedures, or protocols.
> Different—An unexpected deviation from what was planned.

Getting caught doing something DDD, we often find ourselves red faced, looking around in hopes that no one saw. There are usually a few curse words mixed in with phrases such as, "Man, that was stupid!" or "Whoa, I sure was lucky."

Many dumb acts are borne out of our emotions. Target Leaders must maintain a heightened sense of awareness of how emotions drive behaviors.

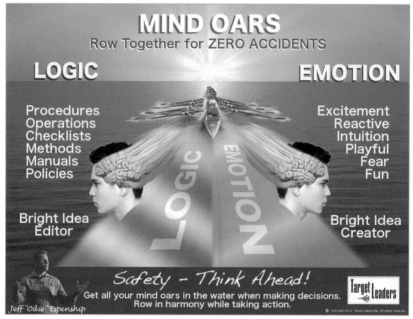

Prevent dumb acts by keeping all your oars in the water.

We have one brain and two minds. Think of your brain like a crew rowboat, and think of your mind like oars sticking out on each side. We have a logical set of oars associated with the left-mind side and an emotional set of oars on the right of our brain boat. To get anywhere safely and efficiently, we need to have both sets of oars in the water, rowing together in relative harmony. The older we get, the more experience we get and the more oars we add to our brain's crew boat.

We need the left set of brain oars for methodical work, logic, checklists, procedures, and rules because the left brain thinks in terms of black and white, cut and dried. When you are balancing your checkbook, you add and subtract numbers with no emotion or creativity (unless you're Bernie Madoff).

We need the right set of brain oars to be creative or to think outside the box. It's the fun, intuitive, and reactive side. It's also the side that is not always accurate. It's the side that tends to get

It is easier to put spilled toothpaste back in the tube than to put spilled words back in our mouth.

us in trouble. Rowing with our emotional oars can send us into circles and make us say things we wished we had not said or do things we later kick ourselves for doing. It's only when we dip our logic oars in the water and begin rowing along in harmony with our emotion oars that we are able to straighten out the brain's emotional circular path.

I bring this up because humans have committed many dumb acts based on emotions. Science tells us that the emotional right side of our brain is the first to jump into action when we are presented with anything fun, dumb, dangerous, or different. This side of the brain recognizes previous patterns. For example, if we see a few employees drop tools into moving pieces of machinery and successfully retrieve the items without shutting down the equipment, then our emotional side of the brain records this information for later use. A month later, when we accidentally drop a screwdriver near a spinning gear, the emotional oars immediately dip into the water, and in an instant we react and reach down to pick the tool up. The problem is that our emotional reactions are not always correct or in our best interests.

When working in high-risk environments, we must slow ourselves down and spend the necessary time, energy, and effort to make sure we dip our logic oars in the water before we act. Keeping our emotional brain in check takes training and discipline. We need to take whatever time is necessary to engage our logical brain and get it in sync before speaking or reacting. Rowing with our logic oars may require us to talk with a trusted friend, coworker, or respected advisor before responding. It may mean rereading the operations manual before we start flipping switches and pushing buttons. Rowing logically may entail running through the checklist a second time or double-checking our work before submitting it for grading.

Because I did not want to delay getting home, I made an emotional snap decision when I told my brother to climb aboard the plane without pulling the propeller through. Had I taken the time to put my logic oars in the water, I would have made the following logical conclusion:

- One pull of the propeller blade takes approximately three seconds.
- For this particular plane, pulling the propeller blade through would require nine pulls of the blade.

- Multiply the two and it would have taken about 27 seconds to execute the procedure properly.

Emotion says, "Let's GO!"

Logic says, "Let's GO—but take a minute to perform the proper procedure first."

There are crimes, and then there are mistakes. The line between the

> *Spend a few seconds of your life doing it right. Otherwise, you can lose your life in a few seconds doing it wrong.*

two is sometimes very thin. Target Leaders have the unenviable task of figuring out which is which when our "children" at home or work have committed a dumb act. Sometimes it helps to understand their intent or what they were thinking when they committed the act. Were they angry? In a hurry? Under pressure? Feeling scared? Apathetic? Trying their best? Not thinking? What did they believe would happen? What results were they trying to accomplish?

Which set of oars were they using when they acted errantly or unsafely? Did they logically decide to not comply with written rules, or was it a spontaneous act? It is really never anyone's intention to cause a brother or sister harm at home or work when rules are broken and dumb acts happen. Many companies establish "golden safety rules" that, if broken, clearly constitute a deliberate unsafe act. This brings up the notion of selective integrity.

"Selective integrity" is an interesting subject Target Leaders should consider when inspiring people to do the right thing. For the most part, we all are honest and want to do what is right. The problem is the difference between what I feel is right, moral, and honest versus what you feel is right, moral, and honest. In some cases, it could be vastly different. Much has been written on the subject of selective integrity, and we could get into a philosophical debate that could lead to another 10 books. That is not my purpose here. However, I think mentioning it is important because it may spark some debate among you as to the reasons why some will selectively adhere to what is right while others do not. Understanding how the people around you think will help you predict their future behavior patterns and hopefully reduce dumb acts personally and professionally.

As a teen, my friends and I loved to joyride around town on Friday night. But the gas in the tank always seemed to run out before our curfew ran out. I was content to go home early and call it a night and then save enough gas money for the following weekend. However, some of my friends had no problem siphoning gas from their neighbors' cars. Personally, I felt this was wrong. It was stealing, so I was never present when they committed such a dumb act. However, I would ride in their car that was being propelled by the gas I considered to be stolen. Selective integrity.

Back then, I lived on Lake Lanier and loved to water-ski. The boat never seemed to have enough gas in it to satisfy my appetite for carving my slalom ski through the glass-smooth water in the early morning hours. Therefore, I had no problem borrowing gas from the neighbor's dock, where there was plenty of gas in cans they used for their Jet Skis. Selective integrity.

In the eyes of the law, these are both crimes. Yet, in my young mind, I felt siphoning gas from someone's car was a crime but "borrowing" gas from our nice neighbor who had gas conveniently in a can was something I could morally justify as a mistake.

As we move into our adult lives, the selective integrity examples continue. In the office, what about taking pens, paper, or rubber bands from the office supply closet and using them at home? What about using the company car for personal use? Company policy may forbid these behaviors, but are the rules enforced?

A Target Leader must stay tuned into the selective levels of integrity being tolerated and the levels being enforced so that there are no mixed messages floating around the shop floor, in the office, or out in the field.

Selective integrity is a close cousin to situational compliance. For example, in the field an employee may use a piece of equipment (forklift, crane, dump truck, etc.) without being properly trained or certified to operate it because he or she wants to help a fellow employee finish a task. Even though company policy forbids using equipment without proper certification, the employee felt the situation called for it. Is this behavior tolerated? What if an accident happens? What then? Crime or mistake?

What about becoming distracted, being complacent, or missing a checklist item that causes the entire job to belly flop? What constitutes a crime to you might constitute a mistake to me. Yet in the battlefield of business, people must understand clearly the level of integrity that is expected of them.

We all have a bit of selective integrity in us, and Target Leaders should leave no doubt as to what is condoned behavior and what is condemned behavior. Whatever level you decide, be consistent in your tolerance and enforcements. Sometimes even rational, logical people allow selective integrity to creep in and influence them to do something dumb-dangerous-different. Only after the mishap do we look back and shake our heads and say, "What a dumb act!"

One area in which to be especially vigilant is when we are working alone. How we behave when we are by ourselves compared with how we are with others may be vastly different. When we work alone, the only check and balance that keeps us on the straight-and-narrow path is our moral character compass. How we operate and what we do without supervision looking over our shoulder pretty much defines our character as an individual. Paying attention to the integrity gaps in our lives will definitely prevent many dumb acts from happening when we are doing things by ourselves.

Fighter pilots rarely fly solo. We have wingmen not only for mutual support but also to keep each other from doing something stupid. Sometimes, though, we are required to fly a solo mission. Many pilots have taken off flying a solo mission, never to return home. The investigation would later determine that the pilot did something that was completely out of character and not normal.

I was speaking to my good friend Danny Raines, founder of Raines Utility Safety Solutions and a regular contributor to *Incident Prevention* magazine. Danny investigated a preventable vehicle accident that happened to a lineman who overturned a brand-new Altec bucket truck on the highway. Luckily, no one was killed, but there were injuries. Danny said the lineman was "the best in his class" when he graduated from the Smith System driving school, but when he operated the vehicle by himself, all the procedures and rules went out the window—literally. The troopers found the driving school manual on the roadside after the crash. Danny mentioned that other employees had witnessed this lineman's poor driving behaviors but they failed to say anything to him about his errant habits. That is a failure in individual leadership among all those who witnessed the poor behavior but did not say something.

"Two peas in a pod" is a metaphor that derives its meaning from the fact that two peas in the same pod are the same or nearly indistinguishable from each other. Several individuals working together as one unit can become as two peas in a pod when no one is looking over their shoulder. How they operate as a single team when no one is looking defines their work culture.

Commercial airlines have jump seats in the cockpit where observers ride along and watch how well the pilots work together as a crew when operating the airplane. Observers such as the FAA are looking for trend items and leading indicators that might forecast a future problem at the airline. I remember a time when an FAA inspector was riding in our jump seat. He said, "I'm not here looking to pick fly crap out of pepper. I'm here to look at the big picture." For anyone tasked with observing others, that makes a lot of sense. He was not there to nitpick us; he was there to observe the broad view. By watching our techniques and procedures and comparing how we operated as one, he learned a lot about how the entire company operated as one.

As a whole, how we fly the airplane when the observer is sitting in the jump seat versus how we operate the jet without someone watching our every move should be exactly the same. In any organization, when there is a difference between the two, that indicates a gap between what is done and what should be done. That is what I call the "selective integrity gap." That means we will do what is right when the observer is there and then do what we feel is right when the observer is not there. The gap can be as thin as a thread or as wide as a crater. The wider the selective integrity gap, the greater the likelihood someone will fall into it and commit a dumb act. Target Leadership in any organization should inspire every individual—all the peas in the pod—to pay attention to the selective integrity gaps, cracks, and fissures that can develop when we are out there working.

Listen carefully for the phrase "I'll be careful." Hearing that phrase is often a gap precursor. It means someone is about to do DDD, probably without thinking it through logically. The selective integrity gap can get really wide if you hear someone say, "Hold my beer and watch this!" How we respond when we hear phrases like that will directly impact our selective integrity gap. If you say "WAIT! Let me get my camera!" then you are helping to widen a gap that others may fatally fall through later on.

However, if you say, "WAIT! Let's think this through!" then you are slowing things down to get the logic oars in the water. To be most effective at inspiring others to make better decisions, we should periodically reflect inward on the gaps within our own lives. Hopefully, this may spark some debate among your fellow Target Leaders about selective integrity gaps and how to keep them closed not only among ourselves but also within ourselves.

After a dumb act, isn't it a shame when we hear someone say, "I knew it"?

I Knew It

Imagine yourself overseeing a fairly complex job that involves a lot of people handling a lot of high-dollar pieces of equipment with a lot of moving parts. You are working through the daily schedule pressures, the standard communication and language barriers, and the ever-present egos when your cell phone rings. "Hello?"

It's your field supervisor. In an agitated tone, he says, "We have an injury on the widget platform!" Your heart sinks. Your mind races. You blurt out, "Who was it?"

There's a brief pause, and then in a measured tone the supervisors says, "Guess who it was?"

A name immediately pops into your mind, and you say it. Come to think of it, it's not really a guess because your answer did not finish with a question mark; instead, the name you guessed was laced with expletives that ended with an exclamation point.

After you blurt out the name, your supervisor replies in a calm voice, "Yup, that's the one." You can almost hear him shaking his head over the phone.

You join him in shaking your head back and forth. "I knew it."

Conversations like this happen all the time, in all industries, all around the globe. In nearly every failed situation, no matter how big or small, all too often we hear someone say, "I knew it." What a shame. As Target Leaders, you and I should be on a personal mission to sniff out all those "I knew it" moments associated with the people and the scenarios before we actually have to say those words.

Questions to think about:

- Is there an improvised tool that people in the field always use to *get-er-done*, a tool that everyone knows is the wrong one but they say "I'll be careful" just before they use it?
- Is there a policy or procedure that people consistently blow off, pencil-whip, or sidestep when they really shouldn't?
- Is there an apprentice or even a seasoned veteran who has a gunslinger attitude when he or she is working either alone or with others?
- Is there a particular group of individuals that when they get together, they roll like loose cannons on the deck of a pitching warship?

THE EGO OF THE "300-HOUR FIGHTER PILOT"

The "300-hour fighter pilot" is a metaphor used in a fighter squadron, and I think it is applicable when trying to stay ahead of "I knew it" situations at work and home. The phrase is used by squadron leadership and refers to a specific group of individuals whose egos have the greatest potential of exceeding their ability, causing harm to themselves or others. For us, this usually occurred with the magic number of having acquired about 300 hours of flight time. It was the most dangerous time for a fighter pilot. Basically, a 300 hour fighter pilot can best be described as one who has just enough experience to think he or she knows everything, but in reality they really don't know____. Well, I won't say it but you smell what I'm stepping in.

They were the group whose ego and self-confidence would most likely lead to an "I knew it" moment.

Your 300-hour fighter pilots might be your apprentices. Maybe they are the employees who have finally completed the months of methodical and arduous training necessary to finally become qualified or licensed to perform their trade. They might be the individual contributors who work alone, doing it their way instead of the correct way. When the 300-hour fighter pilots' egos begin to fly higher or faster than their abilities, the results are often, shall we say, "impacting." Those who *fail* to understand the importance of keeping their "ego ability" in line with their "actual ability" are destined to *feel* the impact of misunderstanding it—sooner or later.

Let me caveat by saying that having a healthy ego and self-confidence is vital to flying high-performance jets, especially in challenging and dynamic situations. Many of you also work in very dynamic and challenging environments, and if not for your high level of confidence, you would not be able to do what you do. Climbing power poles, painting bridges, working on high-rise buildings, or drilling for oil is not for the faint of heart. For any of us, having a healthy ego is essential to thinking positive, being focused, and getting results.

Ego gives you the drive to show the world where you are going and how you do it. Without an ego, the world shows you where to go and how to do it.

Ego is about *believing* in yourself. When you believe in yourself, the impossible becomes your specialty. You could sell fleas to a used-camel salesman if you wanted to! You could inspire a pack of wild dogs to climb down from a meat wagon if you so desired. You could sell ice to an Eskimo.

My 300-hour fighter pilot "I knew it" moment started like all the other days: routine. It was February 1989 when I was stationed at Eielson AFB in Fairbanks, Alaska. I was flying the venerable A-10 "Warthog" on a training mission. I failed to keep my ego ability in line with my actual ability.

I was flying down the frozen Yukon River on a low-altitude tactical navigation (LATN) training mission and was cruising along at 300 feet and 400 mph, approximately half a mile in trail of my flight leader. Suddenly, my radio crackled with his voice: "Odie! Sled dog team ahead."

The 1989 Iditarod sled dog race happened to be taking place, and three-time champion Susan Butcher was defending her title that year. Millions of T-shirts were sold exclaiming, "Alaska—where men are men and women win the Iditarod."

When my flight leader announced that a sled dog team was just ahead, I thought to myself, "I've got to get it on video." The A-10 I was flying that day happened to have a practice B Model Maverick missile mounted on a pod underneath the wing. A practice missile of this type functions only while attached to the airplane. It has no propellant or explosives, but all the switchology, video camera, and missile logic works so we can practice locking up targets. After we land, we can review the gun camera film to measure our successes of locking up targets.

Maverick Missile under the wing of A-10.

When my flight leader announced that he had just flown over a sled dog team, my ego ability piped up and said, "It's perfectly within your ability to lock up and film this sled dog team." Doing this was not part of the plan, and it was not included as part of the prejob briefing. My confidence and perceived skill to operate a fast-moving piece of equipment in a very short amount of time overcame my sense of good judgment. I had to quickly bring up the eyes of the missile (the "eyes" of the missile are its internal camera system), find where it was looking, and then slew its eyes directly over the sled dog team. I had to do this while flying the jet down the valley with high terrain on both sides and also focus on the TV monitor inside the cockpit. The whole time I was doing this, I remember thinking, "I'll be careful." Remember that phrase? It is a precursor to doing something dumb, dangerous, or different!

I locked the eyes of the missile squarely on the sled dog team and began filming. I remember looking at the TV monitor inside the cockpit and staring intently at the sled dog team. I had never seen anything like that before. I am originally from Florida!

I became so enamored with watching the TV screen inside my cockpit that I failed to watch what was happening outside. I was completely oblivious to the surrounding mountains and trees approaching me at more than 400 mph.

Close up of A-10 Cockpit showing location of TV monitor as Odie remained heads down, almost too long, as he views the sled dog team just ahead.

Have you ever been driving and dropped a French fry? Because you are competitive and hate to lose at anything, you are determined to find it. You go heads down a little too long when all of a sudden your internal

alarm clock begins sounding the self-preservation alarm bells, really loud—
"LOOK UP!"

My internal safety timer went off louder than being heads down
texting and driving: "Hey, dummy! LOOK UP!" I looked up, and what
I saw was an underwear-changing scene. A ridgeline moving my way at
400 mph. "D'oh!" It was like looking up and seeing an entire row of
semitrucks stopped dead in the road directly in front of me.

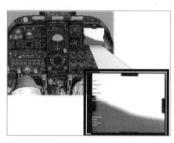

**Picture of the ridgeline that
Odie flewover as he performed
a maximum climbing turn.**

"OH!" Max power! Pull back on the control stick! Turn! Lady luck,
please don't fail me now! If you have ever seen an A-10 perform at an air
show, then you have seen the incredible flying capability of the airplane. I
managed to clear the ridgeline mere seconds before my body became "pink
mist" scattered in a pile of wreckage on the mountain slope.

My ego ability lured me into a situation that pure luck and the
incredible capability of the A-10 pulled me out of. Had I hit the mountains,
can you imagine the phone call that may have taken place?

Ring, ring.

"Hello?"

"Hey! Did you hear? We lost an A-10 today! One fatality!"

"Oh, NO! Who was it?"

"Guess who it was."

"Was it Odie?"

"Yup. That's the one."

"Ohhh, man. I knew it."

I'm sure the headlines in the newspaper would have read: "Fighter
pilot killed today while on a routine training mission."

When squadron leadership found out about what happened, I was quickly in the colonel's office doing "the carpet dance" and trying to explain the dumb act I tempted myself into that day.

Today, I share my sled dog story and show the compelling video that goes along with it to corporate senior leaders, EHS (environment, health, and safety) mangers, and company employees worldwide. I want the audience to figure out who the "300-hour fighter pilots" are in their work life and home life. I want to inspire each of them to have the courage to speak up and say something to their brother or sister before the accident, instead of saying "I knew it" after the accident.

Day in and day out, routine jobs become less safe if we allow our ego to believe that our personal skill, knowledge, and experience are better than what the plan, procedure, or job briefing calls for. Neither the plan nor the briefing called for me to practice Maverick missile lockups on a sled dog team while flying in a valley at 400 mph. That routine training mission almost came to an abrupt halt because I allowed my *confidence to exceed my ability.*

Target Leaders know that overconfidence left unchecked will eventually turn into arrogance. Arrogant people fail to learn, listen, and grow. In their mind they are eight feet tall and bulletproof. They are never wrong. They fight to *be* right, not for *what* is right. Target Leaders understand that *people will operate at the level that is tolerated.* My commanding officer quickly refocused my attitude and work behavior to operate at a much higher level—what is expected, not accepted. Hearing the words "I'll be careful" means that someone is about to rationalize away proven methodologies and correct procedures in order to blend proper techniques with personal techniques.

The more you allow employees to blend their own technique with proper procedure, the more diluted your safety culture becomes. I call this "technique blending." Your work and your surroundings can be just as dangerous and hazardous as flying a fighter jet. As experienced, confident, and professional people, we know that technique blending by others can create an unpredictable work environment. There is not a rule or tool invented

Believing you are able to achieve the task and being able to achieve the task are two very different concepts.

that will protect us if we believe our personal technique is better than what is proven methodology.

—◦◊◦—

In flying, I have learned that carelessness and overconfidence are usually far more dangerous than deliberately accepted risks.

**—Wilbur Wright in a letter to his father,
September 1900**

—◦◊◦—

When we fall for a temptation, it ceases to be a temptation; it's a decision. However, before we make our temptation decision, we usually ponder a few "believe" questions, such as:

- Do I believe I can do this and not hurt myself?
- Do I believe it won't cause too much harm to someone or something else?
- Do I believe I can get away with it, or at least blame my actions on something else?
- Do I believe there is too much risk for the reward?
- Do I believe I can live with myself afterward?

Some temptation decisions will flat out kill us if we get caught. Other temptations we fall for may cause us a minor inconvenience, a small fine, or maybe some embarrassment but nothing major—this time. When temptations are knocking at our door, how we respond ultimately defines us as individuals, as a team, and even as a company.

> *Target leaders inspire us to be responsible for our decisions. Judges hold us responsible for our decisions. Be responsible, not held responsible!*

Being responsible means anticipating ahead of time all those areas at work and home where we find ourselves being tempted to make a wrong choice. This means thinking through and understanding all the future ramifications of our actions. Once these future areas are identified, set an expectation of how you will conduct yourself when the temptation arises. I call this "temptation-expectation."

This means taking the time each day to methodically think ahead and anticipate your weak areas. A lot of convincing serpents hang out in our personal gardens, and you already know where many of them are. They constantly are enticing you to do something dumb, dangerous, or different. By anticipating the "who," "what," and "where" temptation weak areas ahead of time, we have the opportunity to formulate a plan of action. By formulating a plan of action in advance, we can make decisions and set expectations regarding how we will handle future temptations when they pop up. For example, think about the many temptations you face when driving your car: eating, putting on makeup, speeding, not wearing a seat belt, shaving, reading the paper, texting, etc. Think about the errant temptations you face when you are working by yourself versus when you are working with others. Do you act the same, or is it different? Think about the temptations you may knowingly or unknowingly influence in others around you.

When temptation meets expectation, which path will you take? I am far from perfect, and I fall short far more often than I care to admit. But employing the temptation-expectation technique helps me make responsible decisions.

As Target Leaders, it is our duty to anticipate future temptations our fellow employees may face in order to eliminate "I knew it" events. Thus, it is critical that frequent and open discussions take place with them about not only what they perceive as threats but also ways to mitigate the threats. When I was flying A-10s in the air force, investigators later determined that several crashes were a result of the pilot showing off in front of family or friends. Air force senior leadership wanted to remove the temptation of any pilot showboating in front of family when flying solo cross-country. As a result, we were not allowed to fly any cross-country flights that took us within 100 miles of where we grew up or where our parents lived unless we had specific authorization. The problem went away. When temptations get highlighted, they get our attention. What gets our attention gets fixed, and the problem often slithers away to an easier potential victim.

Think of all the well-respected, conscientious people who have been hurt or killed in the line of work because they felt the need to show off their superior skill to a fellow employee or subordinate. Think of the pressure we put on ourselves to get something done ahead of schedule or maybe to please the boss and win favor with the company. Instead, we end up causing a mishap because too many rules were being skirted.

An executive at a large utility power company told me their biggest temptation-expectation moments come when the power goes out. They feel a lot of pressure to get the city lights back on. Everyone jumps into action. How fast they can restore power used to be the measure of success. Not anymore. The measure of success now is how fast they can get the lights on and follow all the safety rules and proper company procedures. Target Leaders within the company have a good idea of how long it should take to get everything done properly. Therefore, if a crew goes out and restores the power in record time, then one of two things happened: they broke a lot of procedures to get 'er done or they discovered a better way of getting 'er done. Either way, it is the Target Leader's job to figure out which is which.

A temptation-expectation moment I can identify came with flying my own airplane. To help me keep up with all my speaking engagements, I bought a Beechcraft Baron airplane. This light twin-engine airplane comfortably cruises at 200 mph and is perfect for landing at small airports close to my speaking venues. Invariably, I face the temptation to fly at night and in bad weather to get to the next speaking destination. Just because the airplane is capable of flying in those conditions and I am licensed to fly on instruments does not mean it is a wise decision to fly myself in those conditions.

A temptation confronted me when I had speaking commitments in different states, with dates and times so close together, that the only way I could make it was to fly myself from one event to the other. No commercial flights were available. The one time I flew in bad weather at night was the one time the heading system went out, which was tied to the autopilot. Now I am hand flying the airplane: single pilot, navigating, talking on the radio, heading system spinning erratically—and I have an hour to my destination. Eventually, I landed safely and had a mechanic fix the problem. I realized that if man were meant to fly, God would have given him wings or more money. Since I had neither, I eventually sold my airplane. I now fly commercially or drive.

When I drive and come to a yellow light at an intersection, I face the temptation of pushing the skinny pedal instead of the fat pedal. Why? Because when I was growing up, my father influenced me to think that "yellow" meant go faster. The opportunity to stop comes once, but the potential for an accident knocks constantly. Now, I anticipate the yellow light temptation to not go faster, and my expectation is to stop when I see one.

Does our will power always hold up when an anticipated temptation bumps up against our expectation? Do I always stick with my game plan and make the agreed-upon or "expected" decision I made with myself ahead of time? Not always. I'm not perfect. Whomever I try to blame or whatever excuse I try to make for falling short, well, all that falls short too. But what is interesting to me is this: when I do fall short and make the wrong decision, my guilty conscience rides me. What results is that I do a better job next time at making the right decision. I become stronger and more resilient. I run fewer yellow lights. I put my phone on "silent" when I get in the car. I wear my seat belt. I do not take shortcuts at work. I keep my ego ability in check with my actual ability. My tolerance for risk is much lower. I will err on the safe side because I want to inspire those around me to do the same. When our people complete a job on time and under budget and follow the rules, we like to say "I knew it" in a good way instead of a bad way.

EIGHT

WATCH YOUR
ATTITUDE

When pilots are flying in conditions that obscure the horizon, the only way they can keep the airplane upright is by referencing the attitude indicator. The attitude indicator itself is located in the center of the instrument panel, directly in front of the pilot. In bad weather, this instrument is considered the life-and-death indicator. Fail to watch it and the attitude of the airplane will tumble out of control in a hurry. Throughout flight instrument training, my instructor pilot admonished me many times to "watch your attitude." He was not referring to my personal attitude; he was directing me to do a better job at keeping the airplane's attitude properly oriented for that particular phase of flight.

Watching your attitude when flying an airplane is analogous to watching your personal attitude. When the weather is great and the sun is shining and we can see for miles around, our attitude is usually pretty good. Pilots would much rather fly in good weather than in bad; it's easier. When the weather turns dark and gloomy, that's when we really have

71

to watch our attitude. This is the time when our energy and focus need to be centered directly in front of us. Fail to watch your attitude carefully and, just as in a real airplane, things can spin out of control in a hurry.

Not only does our attitude have everything to do with us personally but also it has everything to do with us professionally. You're not hired for your job one day and then suddenly become a professional the next. Your employer considered your experience and expertise and hired you as a professional. Being a professional is not a destination that you finally reach; it is an attitude. It's not about the job title; it's about how you do your job. Even though the following jobs are equal, the difference is the professional attitude of the individual doing the work. Which one are you?

There is the babysitter, and then there is the child-care provider who enriches children's minds.

There is the doctor who treats symptoms, and then there is the doctor who focuses on the entire picture of health and wellness.

There is the pilot who complains about having to fly people, and then there is the airline pilot.

There is the cook, and then there is the chef.

There is the person who answers complaints, and then there is the customer service agent.

The list can go on and on. The difference between these jobs is the professional attitude of the individual doing the work.

Watch your attitude.
Your life centers on it.

No one watched his attitude more than my former air force ROTC commander, Colonel Tony "Crusher" Cushenberry. There are people who lead, and then there are Target Leaders. He was a Target Leader. There are people who fly fighters, and then there are fighter pilots. He was a fighter pilot. Crusher's motto was simply this: "'Fighter pilot is an attitude."

He had a fighter pilot's attitude, and he inspired others to adopt a fighter pilot's attitude as well. He was competent but humble, aggressive but smart, rigid but flexible, serious but witty. He wasn't called "Crusher" for nothing. He was a big man who had been an all-American middle linebacker when he played football on scholarship at the University of Georgia. After graduating from Georgia, he joined the air force and went on to fly F-105 Thunderchief fighters out of Thkhli Air Base in Thailand.

He flew more than 125 combat missions against heavily defended targets in North Vietnam and was awarded the Distinguished Flying Cross. He later became the "top gun" in the F-105 while stationed in Spangdahlem, Germany. Crusher was again named top gun among his peers while stationed at Seymour Johnson AFB, in North Carolina, this time while flying the F-4 Phantom. His flying career continued to blossom as an instructor pilot stationed at MacDill Air Force Base, Florida. Then, in 1973, Crusher volunteered for a second combat tour in Southeast Asia. He had survived his first tour in combat, so I asked him why he volunteered for a second. He said pilots make a lot of mistakes during their first tour, and by volunteering to come back again, he hoped to save them from making many of the same mistakes he made during his first tour. He served with distinction.

In 1983, when it was time for Crusher's final assignment before retirement, the air force sent him back to his alma mater as the commander of the University of Georgia Air Force Reserve Officer Training Corps (AFROTC) program. That was where I first met Col. Cushenberry. In 1983, I was beginning my sophomore year in the AFROTC program. At that time, the Georgia ROTC unit was rated number two in the nation. That is, *number two from the bottom* of the list when compared to all other college ROTC programs across the nation. The morale of the place was down, and the attitudes of the staff and the corps of cadets needed "adjusting." Col. Cushenberry brought a fighter pilot's attitude to the anemic program.

My grade point average at that time was a dismal 1.9. On a 4.0 scale, that is definitely below average. It was also well below my abilities, and I knew it! When I began my sophomore year, I remember walking into the ROTC building one afternoon and finding a handwritten note in my cadet mailbox. It simply read, "See me!" There was no question who had left it. The note came straight from Colonel Cushenberry. What was this about? I wondered. I knew I had not done anything spectacular, other than spectacularly goof off. I figured Crusher probably wanted to discuss my grades.

Reading that note made my "pucker factor," a measure of fear-induced tightening of a certain nether region of the anatomy, begin to rise. I put on my dress blue uniform to report to the colonel's office. My pucker factor was about a 9 out of 10, nearly as high as it was when my engine quit while I was flying that summer in Myrtle Beach. At the appointed time, I entered his office, saluted sharply, and stood at attention in front of his big mahogany desk. I tried to remain calm and collected on the outside, but on the inside I was shaking like a Chihuahua on espresso. Through my peripheral vision I noticed that every square inch of wall space in his office was covered with achievement plaques, awards, ribbons, medals, valor certificates, and jet memorabilia. Holy crap, I thought. This is the best "I love me" wall I've ever seen.

"At ease," he commanded without looking up from his desk. He sat quietly. I kept my head still, but my eyeballs couldn't help but rove the walls of his office. My brain felt frozen as I tried to drink in the trappings of success, professionalism, and leadership. I didn't realize he was aware of what I was doing, but he knew. This was Target Leadership by design. He waited until my eyes rested on something of interest. As they fell on a map of Korea, his face softened. Crusher got up from behind his desk and walked over to the map.

In a fatherly tone, he spoke. "I remember sitting at home one evening with my pj's on, watching TV with my kids," he said looking at the map on the wall. "My telephone rang. Our squadron was needed immediately, right here in Kunson, Korea." He tapped the map with his meaty index finger and then turned to me matter-of-factly and said, "Within 48 hours of watching TV with my family, I was landing an F-4 Phantom fighter in Kunson."

I stood nearly speechless, able to utter only a soft "Wow." How on earth do you scramble an entire fighter squadron and get it safely half a world away on a moment's notice? I wondered.

Crusher returned to his desk and picked up my less than average grade sheet.

The softness of his demeanor faded back into concern. "So you want to be a fighter pilot?" he asked.

Silence filled the air, the same gripping silence that filled my cockpit when I ran that tank out of gas—only this time I didn't yell out "OH!" In as enthusiastic a voice as I could muster, I said, "Yes, Sir! More than anything." He leaned forward slightly, looked me square in the eyes, held up my below-average grade sheet in his big right hand, and said, "Well, my air force does not have below-average fighter pilots."

BANG! Down came the gavel.

In that moment, I shrank, just like I did after telling Dennis I had run the right tank out of gas. If I had the tallest ladder in the world, it would still not have been tall enough for me to reach up and tickle the belly of a worm. Crusher held my entire future, my whole aviation career, in that big right hand of his. He was judge, jury, and executioner of my destiny to become a fighter pilot. My subpar grade sheet he was holding was all the evidence he needed to overturn my aspirations of flying in the air force. What was I thinking? All those nights goofing off could have been spent far more wisely doing something useful, like studying!

A Target Leader's job is to figure out how to inspire the desire in others to believe and achieve a high level of excellence, to perform beyond their current level, and to rise above the standard they have set for themselves. That day in his office, Crusher gave me one of the greatest "watch your attitude" instructional talks I've ever received, witnessed, or given. He inspired me to believe in myself and achieve excellence. This carried me not only for the rest of my time in college but also for the rest of my life.

He talked about how I had accepted below-average grades as being "good enough." We have all received less than average evaluations, but how we choose to accept below-average grades says a lot about our attitude. Crusher was not going to let me get away with allowing myself to accept a less than average personal performance when we both knew my ability was much higher. No more accepting the college party mantra of "if the minimum wasn't good enough, it wouldn't be the minimum." That is not the fighter pilot's attitude. Not in college, not in life, not in Crusher's air force!

Watching your attitude is not about being perfect; it's about the pursuit of constant improvement. Some people have tremendous heart and a warrior's spirit, yet despite their very best efforts to improve, they have reached the end of their talent rope. Even then, their attitude does not allow them to quit or give up. These are the people we root for the hardest because they are constantly trying to improve and their efforts inspire us to do better as well. More than half of the students washed out of my air force pilot training class despite their very best efforts. They just did not have the talent or the ability to fly jets.

On the other side of the coin, some people have God-given talents, yet they perform at a level beneath their ability. These are the people we want to shake because we see them wasting their talent. The Target Leader's job is to do some inspirational tail kicking to get them to perform at a higher level, like Crusher did to me. By the end of my sophomore year, I made the dean's list with a 3.8 GPA. Col. Cushenberry challenged and inspired our entire AFROTC unit's performance to rise to its true level of ability. Under his Target Leadership, our detachment was chosen as the top unit among all 36 units in the southeastern United States. That same year, out of all 158 detachments in the nation, we rose to number two—this time from the top. We stayed at the top until Crusher retired.

The attitude adjustment wasn't the only bit of inspiration I got that day in Crusher's office. Upon leaving, I saluted sharply, did an about-face, and began to walk out the door. Before I hit the threshold, his commanding voice said, "Espenship! One more thing."

I stopped dead in my tracks, did another about-face, and asked, "What's that, Sir?"

"I want you to have this Plexiglas navel," he said, tossing me a round piece of plastic about two inches in diameter. I held it for a moment, thinking I might find some clue as to what the heck it was.

Crusher timed his remark perfectly. Serious but witty, he pointed to it and said with a smirk, "Fighter pilots use their Plexiglas navel so that when they get their head stuck up their butt, they can still look out and see where they are going."

I smiled broadly. Not only was he a great leader but also he had a sense of humor that put me at ease in his presence. A bit of humor in stressful situations can be a powerful tool to make people more comfortable and put them in a better position to learn.

I took the fighter pilot's Plexiglas navel to the next level and made replicas into key chains with the words "Plexiglas navel" embossed on the top. I often use these as a communication tool and a conversational icebreaker when I see someone about to do something dumb, dangerous, or different. Offering up a Plexiglas navel helps me start an important conversation in a lighthearted way.

Sometimes, when I'm speaking at corporate events, I bring a big bag of Plexiglas navels and hand them out to the audience after telling my story. They're always a big hit. When I have revisited companies years later, employees have reached into their pockets and pulled out their Plexiglas navel keychain and said, "Hey, Odie, I still carry my Plexiglas navel!" I pull mine out and say with a smile, "So do I."

—⁓—

As of this writing, my son Michael is a chemistry major at the University of Georgia. He has a God-given talent and true ability to comprehend such a difficult subject. He also works very hard, studies intently, and prepares for every test. Because of that, he makes As. Rarely does he make a B, but when he does, he may be a little disappointed, but he's never down or dismayed. He knows he gave his maximum effort, and he can't ask any more of himself than that. His diligence inspires me to reach higher, and for that he is a Target Leader.

—⁓—

When I was flying A-10s, I participated in a very intense two-week military war game called Red Flag. This is an exercise where Blue Forces, consisting of air and ground crews from the air force, navy, and marines, as well as forces from the North Atlantic Treaty Organization (NATO) and other allied countries, train in real combat situations against an enemy known as the Red Forces. The Red Forces are composed mostly of Americans trained to use enemy tactics and actual enemy hardware against us good guys, the Blue Forces. As Blue Force fighter pilots, our job was to plan and fly missions against the very seasoned and highly skilled Red Force enemy.

If poor performance is not corrected immediately, future performance will eventually sink below the current level being tolerated.

All flying was done within the vast Nevada Test Training Range at Nellis Air Force Base. We used live ammunition against ground targets whenever possible to accurately simulate combat. This made the war game intensely realistic.

Our Blue Forces commander was the legendary Lieutenant Colonel Joe-Bob Phillips. He had absolutely no tolerance for poor performance. He was tall and sinewy with piercing slate gray eyes and salt-and-pepper hair. Years as a hardened fighter pilot mixed with an after-hours love of whiskey and cigars had ground his voice to a deep, gravelly rasp that made fighter pilots listen. That distinct deep voice was immediately recognizable when he spoke on the radio, too.

In the morning briefing on the first day of the exercise, before anyone had turned a wheel, LTC Phillips stood in front of all 400 Blue Forces fighter pilots in the main auditorium and took the opportunity to clearly define his expectations for each of us in the room. His number one expectation was *zero* incidents. This was the first time I heard a senior leader set such a high expectation for a job that large and intense. He did not want one single incident from any of us. How can that be? I thought. If we train like we plan to fight, then we will fight like we were trained, and a few incidents always come along with realistic training. It's just part of the deal, right?

I was all of 26 years old, a freshly minted fighter pilot, whispering to the guy sitting next to me, "I understand an expectation of zero fatalities. But, come on, zero accidents? No way! There are too many knuckleheads in this room—myself included—who will eventually mess up or do something dumb, dangerous, or different." He nodded in agreement, especially at the knucklehead part.

Many companies allow for a certain number of incidents, accidents, or even fatalities per number of hours worked. It's plain statistics. At the end of the year, if fewer people died than were statistically estimated, then woo-hoo, the company met its goal of killing fewer people than expected. Red Flag was no different. The anticipated loss rate was seven accidents per 100,000 flight hours. It could be a procedural misstep, minor switch error, moment of inaction or indecision, checklist omission, task overload, loss of situational awareness, complacency, channelized attention, or any of a hundred other human behaviors that lead to fatalities. LTC Phillips continued to outline why he set such a monumental expectation of zero incidents for this particular exercise.

With a voice that sounded like tires traveling slowly down a gravel road, he said, "A typical fighter pilot makes an average of 10 screwups in the cockpit per hour." He looked toward a section where a group of marine aviators were sitting and added with a slight grin, "For you marines, that statistic is a bit higher!" There was some laughter from the audience.

Marines are used to the jokes, but when the fighting starts, we are glad to have them on our side.

Phillips continued, "Multiply 10 screwups per hour times 400 fighter pilots in this room. That is 4,000 mistakes made in your collective cockpits per hour! Each of you will fly an average of two hours per day. That's a potential for 8,000 combined mistakes per day, and the exercise is two weeks long."

I leaned over to my wingman sitting next to me and whispered, "In this business, one mistake can easily equal one fatality."

We flew the entire exercise with a fighter pilot's attitude of zero accidents. We finished two weeks later with zero fatalities, which is much better than if we had started with the usual expectation of seven losses per 100,000 flight hours. However, a few incidents did occur. The exercise itself was more than just flying; it became an opportunity for us to set clear and measurable expectations for ourselves at all times. When we fell short, we evaluated how we could have done better and applied those lessons the following day.

By watching our attitude, we help others watch theirs. This ultimately creates a professional culture of constant monitoring, evaluating, and accountability and continuous improvement. Remember to watch your attitude. The little things make the biggest difference.

It's the Little Things

The little things matter. If you don't believe me, try sleeping with a mosquito in the room or walking around with a pebble in your shoe. Ask a blue whale how he grew so big. He will tell you, "Plankton, the little things."

For you and me, it's the little things that make the difference between crying "Whaah!" or exclaiming "Wow!" While we pilots are sitting at the gate prior to push back with the cockpit door open, passengers sometimes pay us a visit. Their first impression is just to stare at all the switches and dials with mouths agape. Sometimes they utter a soft "Woooow" in the same wonderment as I did that day I stood in Col. Cushenberry's office and listened to him talk about flying to Korea. They wonder how a person can know what every switch does, what each dial means, and how to fly this machine at the same time.

The answer is simple. It's about the little things. Pilots make sure every little thing is put in the correct position at the appropriate time.

When we arrive safely at our destination, we put all those little things back in their original position for the next operating crew. When you think about it, what you do at work is very similar to what a commercial pilot does. You do your job, or finish a shift, by successfully doing a whole bunch of little things sequentially and correctly, which ultimately yields positive results.

Basically, everything good in life boils down to the little things. Grand accomplishments do not happen because of one enormous event. The successful events are the result of the steady drip-drip-drip of doing the little things right. The aggregation of incremental successes is what carries us safely and productively through the years. Super Bowls are won when one team consistently accomplishes an aggregate succession of little things throughout the entire season better than all the other teams. One giant leap may have put a man on the moon, but millions of little steps got us there. Winning and losing in life and leadership are the same way. They are a succession of little things.

It's the small switch error, a slight distraction, or the misreading of a pressure gauge that causes many untimely job endings. Something that may seem little at the time can end up causing some of our biggest problems. Reactively reaching into a moving piece of equipment to retrieve a dropped item may seem like a little thing at the time, until you lose your limb or life. Then it's a significant life event, for everyone.

After an accident, when we are asked to recount what happened, many people associated with the mishap lament how the job was going *routinely*. That's how it is, isn't it? One minute we are all relaxed and doing our little routine job with our brain blissfully on autopilot, and in a split second we find ourselves caught completely off guard. The first sign of trouble that something small is turning into something big usually comes from a coworker or someone in the vicinity. A short statement from them such as "OH!" clues us in. The next thing we witness is the reaction. It's like walking into a spider web. Your body instantly transforms itself into a black belt karate ninja who uses lots of swear words. The littlest things can cause the biggest reactions, sometimes the biggest laughs, and sometimes the worst disasters.

If we successfully manage the little things, the big things will take care of themselves.

The idea is to pay attention to all the little routine spiderwebs that are slowly and quietly being built around us that cause crazy reactions when we inadvertently walk into them. Your job may seem routine to you now, but think back to when you were first learning. Things were not so routine then. You kept a sharp eye out for all the cobwebs. You were careful not to be caught off guard, and you were not complacent. You spoke up and asked questions.

I clearly remember sitting in the cockpit of the air force jet trainer for the first time and staring at all those switches, dials, and gauges. The look on my face was like that of a monkey staring at a wristwatch: amazed confusion. "Woooooow," I thought. "The day the air force lets me fly this thing is the day it had better ground all the other jets."

Slowly and methodically, though, I learned. It wasn't pretty, but one of the best at training a monkey like me how to fly was my instructor pilot, Scotty Porter. He got me safely through a lot of ugly moments. He was a super sharp guy, having graduated from the U.S. Air Force Academy as a distinguished graduate. He was one of the top instructor pilots at the USAF pilot training base at Vance AFB in Enid, Oklahoma.

Scott Porter handing Odie his coveted silver Air
Force wings after graduating from pilot training.

Scotty was an instructor pilot in the advanced trainer jet called the T-38 Talon. This beautiful supersonic jet is known affectionately as "the White Rocket." Learning to fly that needle-nosed pointy thing was like sitting on the end of a fast-moving pencil. Many times the jet would be flying along at 500 mph, but my brain would be going only about 50 mph.

Even though the jet was fast, Scotty did a great job of slowing things down for me. He was really good at listening my questions, but he answered the question I meant to ask. Staying ahead of the student and knowing the mistakes he or she is going to make before they make it is the hallmark of a good instructor and the secret to longevity.

Think back to a time when you were learning something new. You were very focused and methodical. You paid close attention and worked slowly. I had to do the same as I learned to fly high-performance jets. So many little things demanded my attention, especially when I learned to fly in tight formation while maintaining a scant 3 feet of wing-tip clearance. I remember attempting my first formation flight in the T-38. I was flailing around like a monkey trying to *find* the football, much less do anything noteworthy with it. Learning to fly tight formation while maneuvering is an artful skill that is difficult to learn, but Scotty came through with his slow and methodical teaching style. Formation flying in the T-38 was responsible for many student pilots washing out. Despite having a great attitude and trying really hard, some just could not perform to the minimum standards.

Air force instructor pilots are the best at inspiring students to perform to their maximum ability. Scotty made me pursue perfection on every training flight. Trust me: he did not get perfection from me, but what he did get was excellence. My class started pilot training with 60 student pilot candidates. One year later, only 30 of us graduated! That's right; 50% could not attain the minimum standards and were subsequently washed out. Of the 30 that graduated, I was chosen as the top graduate. This accomplishment was largely due to my instructor, Scotty Porter, who set high expectations of me on every single training flight.

I was very fortunate to have spent time with an instructor like Scotty, who was in charge of teaching me lifesaving skills on a daily basis, and I am deeply appreciative of his efforts. Over the one-year course of pilot training, Scotty and I became good friends. Looking back, as stressful as it was, I had a lot of fun learning to fly jets.

—∿∿∿—

Learning should be fun. If you don't have fun in aviation, then
you don't learn, and when learning stops, you die.

—**Pete Campbell, FAA**

—∿∿∿—

After Scotty's three-year assignment as an instructor pilot in the T-38 at Vance AFB, he was reassigned to fly the F-16 "Fighting Falcon." His dream to become a fighter pilot was realized. He quickly progressed flying the F-16 in his new squadron and became an instructor pilot and a four-ship flight leader. All was going very well for him and his air force career until one day he inadvertently walked into that one little spiderweb that was quietly being built while no one was looking. Unfortunately, Scotty's reactions were not timely enough to save him. It was a little thing, just one switch . . .

Just one little switch out of place in his F-16 that day ended everything. As I reflect on his tragic loss, I am reminded that every one of us has the "one little switch" in our daily cockpit of life. Even though we have all met the minimum standards to be qualified to do our work, if we fail to get the one switch right, a seemingly little thing, it can prove to be devastating—to ourselves, to those around us, to our friends, and to our families. Not only did that one switch kill Scotty but also it killed the person who happened to be riding along in the backseat of the two-seat model F-16 Scotty was flying that day.

Riding in the backseat cockpit that day was the base flight surgeon. He was an aeromedical doctor commonly referred to as the Flight Doc. It is important to note here that he was not a pilot, but as the Flight Doc, he was allowed to occasionally ride along in the backseat of the F-16 if it was available. Scotty's backseat happened to be available that fateful day.

Before I go further, please know that in sharing a few details of this accident, I hope we do not critique their actions or decisions. My prayer is that we glean whatever nuggets of wisdom their untimely deaths may expose. Our job is never to judge, only to learn. Learning from the mistakes of others means hanging their picture in the gallery of our mind and referring to it. Use the gift they gave to clean out the cobwebs of mediocrity, overconfidence, and complacency.

To help us understand how the crash unfolded, some background on the F-16 is required. While the control stick of most fighter jets is located between the pilot's legs, the F-16's control stick is unique in that it is side mounted. It is located on a shelf slightly to the right of the pilot's right knee. It is a comfortable location and an easy reach for the pilot's right hand to control. The way a control stick works is simple; as Scotty used to say, "To make houses look big, push forward. To makes houses look small, pull back."

Pilots refer to the F-16 as "the Electric Jet." I think they should call it the "the PFM Jet" because exactly how it works is PFM—pure freaking magic. The inputs from the side-mounted control stick are sent to an electronic box known as a flight control computer, or FLCC. As the pilot makes inputs via the control stick, the FLCC electronically makes thousands of measurements per second to interpret what the pilot wants to do. Anything that can interpret what a pilot wants to do is magic. The jet magically moves hundreds of exterior flight surfaces to execute the maneuver the pilot wants. The axiom among F-16 pilots is "You don't fly the F-16; it flies you."

Here's something else interesting about the F-16. The side-mounted control stick moves only a quarter inch in any direction. That's it! For example, if the pilot moves the control stick a full quarter inch to the right, the jet will begin rapidly rolling to the right at a rate of two rolls per second! That's right—the roll rate of the F-16 after moving the stick only a quarter inch to the right or left is 520 degrees per second! If you are ever curious to know what that's like, just hop in your washing machine and select the spin cycle.

THE ACCIDENT

Accident investigation revealed that Scotty and the Flight Doc's day started just like all the other days: routine. The purpose of their routine training mission was to practice a low-level bombing run on a ground target at the tactical bombing and gunnery range. This was something Scotty had done many times before, and he was very familiar with how things should operate. Everything was going as planned. Scotty released his practice bombs on time and on target. Bull's-eye! They were egressing down a valley corridor while flying low and fast to simulate staying beneath enemy radar coverage. Flying the F-16 straight and level, especially when low to the ground, requires finesse and very slight hand pressures on the control stick. Scotty and the Flight Doc were about 500 feet high and flying close to 600 mph when all of a sudden, the flight data recorder (recovered from the black box) revealed that the F-16 began to roll very slightly but uncommanded to the right. Scotty immediately countered with opposite left-stick pressure adjustment, which caused the jet to right itself.

As Scotty held left-stick correction, the cockpit voice recorder (recovered from the black box) revealed Scotty calmly saying, "Hey, Doc. Make sure your feet are off the rudder pedals." By saying that, obviously Scotty assumed that the Doc was keeping his hands clear of the control stick. Scotty thought maybe the Doc was pushing inadvertently with his feet on the rudder pedals, which would in fact make the jet roll slightly.

However, when Scotty queried the Doc to make sure his feet were off the rudder pedals, the jet rolled rapidly to the right. Now they were completely upside down. Scotty reacted quickly with 100 units (a full quarter inch) of left-stick pressure, in hopes the jet would roll back left in order to right itself. The jet did not respond to Scotty's full left-stick pressure. Now inverted, down low, and out of control, Scotty suspected a complete failure of the "magic" FLCC. As the ground was whizzing by his canopy at 10 miles per minute, Scotty initiated dual seat ejection. Unfortunately, the plane was outside the safe operating envelope for the ACES II rocket-powered ejection seat to function properly. The accident report listed the cause of death as "ejection sequence interrupted by ground impact."

A good friend of mine was one of the many on-scene accident investigators. He told me much of the details about what they discovered, but basically all that was found of Scotty was his wallet, a piece of his leather name tag, and the heel from his left flight boot. Hitting the ground at 600 mph doesn't leave investigators very many pieces and parts to examine. However, they found enough to determine exactly what happened.

Re-creating the flight, the investigators revealed that as Scotty was releasing his bombs in the target area, the Doc was making a determined effort to keep his hands clear of the control stick and his feet clear of the rudders. As the jet was egressing low and fast down the valley floor, the Doc was doing such a good job of keeping his feet off the rudder pedals that his right knee was inadvertently pushing very slightly against the side-mounted control stick in his backseat cockpit. This caused the jet to roll very slightly to the right. The Doc did not feel the stick touching his right knee because he was wearing a G suit, which is a suit that fits tightly around the pilot's legs and abdomen. It fills with high-pressured air and is designed to elevate the fighter pilot's blood pressure when performing flight maneuvers.

When the jet began to roll slightly to the right, Scotty made a bit of left-stick correction and said, "Hey, Doc. Make sure your feet are off the rudder pedals." Guess how the Doc responded to that command? He responded in the same manner that anyone would: he simply pulled his feet farther away from the rudder pedals, which caused his right knee to put 100 units (a full quarter inch) of right pressure against the control stick in his backseat cockpit. With that, the jet rolled so quickly to the right that by the time Scotty could react with left pressure up in his front seat, they were already upside down.

So there they were, upside down, close to the ground, going fast. Scotty, in the front cockpit, was commanding the FLCC to roll left at 100 units and at the same time in the back cockpit, Doc was unknowingly commanding the FLCC to roll right at 100 units. What was the FLCC to do? It did nothing. Each input canceled the other. The FLCC may be magic, but it does not work miracles.

The FLCC was functioning correctly all along. That's how it is for those of us who work in high-risk and dangerous work environments. Like Scotty, one minute we are blissfully going through our routine workday, and the next, out of nowhere, we find ourselves caught off guard. Like a knife fight in a telephone booth, you are battling desperately against something you can't see, and you must figure out, or comprehend, what is happening. How things turn out is a matter of luck and reaction. It doesn't have to be that way, though. Figuring out the root causes of accidents like Scotty's will help us stay out of knife fights in phone booths.

After the investigators determined the origin of the accident, they set about finding root causes. The operations manual of the F-16 stated that any time a nonpilot rode in the backseat, the pilot flying the airplane must electronically disable the back stick with *one switch*. That switch is physically located outside the cockpit and is turned off by the F-16 pilot as part of the preflight check. Since the Flight Doc was a nonpilot riding in the backseat, Scotty was supposed to turn the back stick off before flying the training mission. Investigators found that the switch was left in the on position.

Why did Scotty not comply with the procedure? Was he unaware of it? Was he misinformed, or did he misunderstand its purpose? Did he forget about the procedure? Was he in too big of a hurry during his preflight? Did he fall victim to situational compliance?

Since Scotty was an instructor pilot in the F-16, the investigators determined that he knew about the *one switch*. He was neither misinformed of its proper use nor in a hurry, nor did he simply forget about it during his preflight. On the surface, it would seem that the easy thing to do is to blame Scotty, or maybe to some degree the Flight Doc, for this tragic loss of man and machine.

The Blame Game

Remember how easy it is to blame others when things go wrong and how pointing a finger at someone else for our own shortcomings is actually within our DNA? After all, that is what Adam did to Eve when he got caught taking a bite of the apple and Eve in turn blamed the serpent. That is how easy it is to create a culture of blame and how quickly zero accountability begins. This toxic culture is unintentionally created by leaders who, after a failure occurs, begin probing for fault. When this happens, everyone reacts defensively. When the essence of the question asked is "who is at fault?" all fingers will point outward. The squadron could have blamed Scotty, or even the Doc, for not complying with proper procedures. That would be the easy thing to do because they are dead. However, the root cause would still be alive. It did not die with the victim(s). It would lie as still as a serpent in the woods, waiting for its next victim.

Target Leaders wish to avoid blame and finger-pointing. Their mission is to inspire a culture of open communication, responsibility, and inward reflection. Instead of looking for scapegoats, their mission is to inspire us to figure out *how to* prevent the mishap from happening again. This is how we get to the root cause of incidents and accidents. Chopping off the head of the snake is the only way to keep it from striking again. That buries the root problem for good. That is what was done after Scotty's accident.

The investigation determined that any time nonpilots rode in the backseat, the pilot in command allowed them the opportunity to actually fly the F-16. The only way do this was not to disable the back stick. Like many of you working your job or operating your equipment, fighter pilots have a similar high-level degree of confidence in their ability to handle themselves. They believe they can handle any situation a nonpilot attempting to fly the F-16 might try. You might feel the same confidence when you allow your child to sit in your lap and steer the car down a deserted country road.

After much soul searching and inward reflection among all the other pilots in the squadron, they realized that the root cause of Scotty's mishap boiled down to the catch phrase "It's the way we do it around here."

What seemed to be a little thing, one switch, turned out to be a much bigger thing, a culture thing. Too many leaders seemingly were influencing "the way we do it around here" and not enough Target Leaders were influencing "the way we should do it around here."

Nearly every piece of machinery we operate has procedures tested and written by engineers. The job of the operator is simple: learn and comply. To that end, many companies adopt a compliance-based safety system that operates very similarly to that of strict parents who say to their children "Comply or else!" Sometimes that works, but we can never rule out human nature. Despite engineers' or test pilots' best efforts to come up with

Just when you think something is foolproof, you've underestimated the ingenuity of a fool.

correct processes, they cannot think of everything. When somebody gets hurt following proper protocol, a new procedure is introduced. It's said to be "written in blood." Sometimes people do something so foolish the engineers did not dream it possible, much less write a procedure for it. Unfortunately, the next gold nugget is so true.

In many ways, the military is certainly a compliant-based leadership-safety system. Like the military, companies such as yours also want to fix those areas where a reasonably intelligent and skilled person, like a fighter pilot, might be tempted to misbehave and not comply with what is written. To that end, Target Leaders never rule out human error and human behavior. After Scotty's accident, the air force modified the F-16 and created new guidelines allowing nonpilots to actually fly the F-16. The engineers relocated the "one switch" and put it inside the front cockpit and wrote a procedure for its proper use when nonpilots are riding in the backseat of the F-16. Blaming Scotty would not have fixed the problem. When the air force reflected inward as a whole and spoke openly to all the other pilots about the issue, the problem was fixed within the entire organization. Scotty's accident was in 1995, and since that time no other incidents similar to his have occurred.

If our belief was that we could die doing what we are about to do, then our attitudes would change about doing what we just did. Often, we need to change the perceptions about the importance of the little things.

When preparing for a mission in the A-10 or planning a trip as an airline pilot, I was never concerned about the big things. As a pilot, there are two—and only two—BIG rules to follow. Rule number 1 is do not hit the ground. Rule number 2 is do not hit anything attached to the ground. I spent the majority of my time concentrating on the hundreds of little things, and the two big things always took care of themselves. In the same vein, the plant manager at a refinery does not spend his or her time dwelling on whether the entire plant is going to explode. Shift supervisors of manufacturing facilities do not walk around wondering whether someone is going to lose a limb that day. On the road, truck drivers don't believe they are going to have a fatal accident that day. The CEOs of large construction companies do not wring their hands every hour stressing over whether the building their company just built is going to collapse. These are all big things! When we consistently perform the little things above the minimum standards accepted by Target Leadership, then the big things always take care of themselves.

TEN

ENERGY IS LIFE

Fighter pilots who have been trained for air-to-air combat, dogfighting, have a saying: "Energy is life." In a dogfight, our energy bucket is the summation of the aircraft's airspeed (kinetic energy) and altitude (potential energy). In the rough-and-tumble world of dogfighting, our life depends on energy management. How well one pilot manages his or her energy over the other in a dogfight is directly related to winning or losing. One pilot may elect to climb and trade airspeed for altitude while the other elects to dive and trade altitude for more speed. At the same time, one pilot may pull the throttles to idle and extend the speed brakes while the other selects full afterburner for maximum thrust. Like two dogs chasing each other in circles, the opposing fighter pilots twist and turn through the sky, each jockeying for a firing position. Running out of energy first means placing second in a dogfight.

The official term for this tit-for-tat offensive and defensive maneuvering is called ACM, or air combat maneuvering. We call it "turning and burning," and it uses energy, lots of it. Fighter pilots who manage their energy the best and make the fewest mistakes usually win the turning-and-burning contest. Now, this chapter is not about shooting people down. It's about managing our energy, making as few mistakes as possible, and ultimately winning challenges personally and professionally.

Professionally, the business world is a highly competitive arena where companies expend a lot of energy to get on top and stay on top. The better the company and its people manage their energy, the better chance they have at staying competitive and winning. Managing energy means understanding when to conserve assets and when to expend them. Conserving energy may mean taking a break, going on vacation, or asking for help. Expending energy may mean aggressively going after a new client, working overtime to meet a production goal, or rallying the team to push through a hardship. Deciding when to expend valuable resources such as money, personnel, or supplies versus when to conserve those assets for another day requires managerial judgment regarding the use of energy. We will never fly the perfect dogfight, run the perfect business, or be the perfect leader. We will never manage our energy, our assets, or our lives perfectly. At times we will make mistakes, mismanage our energy, fritter away assets, misdirect someone, or fail to act decisively.

Winning personal dogfights in life is not about being perfect, nor is it about dominating others. It's about being in control of our lives. When a fighter pilot takes control of a dogfight, it is called "pushing the fight." This is not about starting the fight; it's about finishing the fight. We all face dogfights daily. Many of us are fighting to get out of debt; some are fighting addictions and temptations. Maybe you are fighting to complete a big project or struggling to fulfill a promise you have made to someone. People fight to find a job, or a better job, or even a promotion. In any challenge you face, remember that pushing the fight means taking control. This means making the challenge react to you instead of you reacting to the challenge. The difference is subtle, but learning to make the challenge react to you is a powerful tool.

While going through ACM training at Holloman AFB in New Mexico, I remember my instructor pilot briefing me on the art of being in control and pushing the fight. During the dogfight

The more you take control, the more your challenges become the challenged.

itself, he sat in the backseat of the AT-38B jet and coached me along as I flew. The more I pushed the fight—managing my energy, expending it, conserving it, and then expending it again—the more control I had.

Target Leaders coach and mentor others to push the fight and win their struggles, just as my instructor pilot helped me push the fight and win the dogfight. Pushing the fight means anticipating what lies ahead and being proactive in order to control the outcome. Take the controls of your flight path and achieve a winning solution; that is self-empowerment. Make things happen instead of hoping or waiting for something to happen. When you empower yourself to start making things happen, energy is expended, and others will notice and react to it. When positive things start happening within a group, the effect becomes synergistic. The team gets caught up in the synergy that is created by proactive people pushing the fight, managing their energy, and making things happen. When these interactive elements combine, the synergistic result creates more energy for the team, the family, and the company.

The total effect of synergy is greater than the sum of the individual elements contributing to it.

When the authors of the first law of thermodynamics stated that "energy can neither be created nor destroyed," they forgot about synergy. Energy is created by team synergy. Energy can also be destroyed by synergy's opposite, "antergy." OK, I made that word up because I could not find an antonym to "synergy" and I needed one to make my point. Antergies are like ants at a picnic—ruinous. When I joined the 18th Tactical Fighter Squadron at Eielson Air Force Base in Fairbanks, Alaska, as a brand-new A-10 fighter pilot, antergies and negative energy abounded in the squadron. Morale was low and getting lower. The entire Air Force Base Wing, including the 18th TFS squadron, had just failed its big operational readiness inspection (ORI). This essentially meant that the entire air base was not up to minimum standards if called upon to deploy and defend our country. To compound the negative energy problem, the 18 TFS squadron itself was still dealing with the recent sad loss of one of their brothers who flew an A-10 into a mountain in bad weather. The relentless cold and darkness of the Alaskan winter were also approaching. This was not the high-energy turn-and-burn atmosphere that I envisioned when joining my first fighter squadron. I expected the squadron to have the synergy of *Top Gun*; instead, it had the antergy of *Flop Gun*.

Speaking of *Top Gun*, I found out that being called Maverick, Iceman, and Viper happens only in the movies. Real call signs for real fighter pilots are more like Grumpy, Boner, Chugger, Tater, Spanky, Egg, Senator, Dahmer, Fido, and Buddha. A call sign pretty much sums up the individual: who he or she is, his or her personality, his or her character traits. In one word, your call sign is the vibe others feel about you, and they tag you with it. It's usually spot-on, and the call sign sticks.

One fighter pilot had a mole on his left cheek, about the size of a small pencil eraser. His call sign was Spot. We had another pilot whose first name was Dane. He made the mistake of requesting that we call him Danger. Instead, we called him Brammage because Dane was surely suffering from "Dane Brammage" for thinking we should call him Danger. Hilarious!

As for my call sign, well, I had boundless energy. I was always eager to fly any mission, anytime, anywhere. The energy I gave off made others think of Garfield's sidekick dog, Odie. My tail was always wagging and my tongue happily hanging out and drooling on everyone's shoes. In a nutshell, you could describe me as a person who had a lot of velocity and a tiny rudder. I was just like the dog Odie, and the call sign stuck. To this day, nobody knows me by my first name, Jeff. Everyone knows me as Odie.

Having boundless energy and a lot of speed is a good thing as long as the rudder is big enough to guide it in the right direction. Target Leaders inspire proper guidance. They give focus, vision, and direction so that the rudder keeps the ship pointed toward the proper destination. Once that happens, Target Leaders can use that fresh energy to breathe new life into the people and the organization. Despite the 18 TFS squadron's morale being in the doldrums, a few Target Leaders there helped steady my tiny rudder. I empowered myself to take the initiative and find a few things that needed improvement. One Target Leader in particular helped support my efforts—our new squadron commander, Colonel Bob Woods.

The newest member of any squadron is always referred to as the FNG (friggin' new guy). As a lowly FNG second lieutenant, I had to watch my step to make sure I did not overstep my bounds or upset too many apple carts. Slowly I began pushing the fight, being proactive. I took the initiative to improve a few little things because the little things matter.

For example, I felt the quick-reference mission data cards that we used could be redesigned with more relevant information. These cards were pre-printed with standard information, and each pilot took one to the prejob briefing and jotted down notes for the upcoming mission. We then strapped the card to our knee for quick reference when we flew. I began by asking my squadron mates for their thoughts for improving the mission data cards. Some said, "There's nothing wrong with the ones we have," while others gave a lot of valuable input. I collected information from all the pilots and implemented the new changes. By the end of the first two weeks of flying, every pilot was using the new cards. Even the naysayers sat up and took notice.

You cannot fix everything, but you can fix something.

Another project that made others sit up and take notice was refurbishing the squadron songbook. This book had traditional fighter pilot songs that dated back to World War II. I had the book reprinted, and I distributed copies to every pilot in the squadron. You got a copy only if you attended "choir practice" held at the informal squadron bar called the Fox Den. The synergy grew week after week as more pilots showed up to get their copy, sing traditional fighter pilot songs, and toast those who had gone before us. The Crud table was moved to the center of the bar. I could feel the energy rise as the synergy began taking over the entire group.

———

Crud is a fast-paced game of skill, team execution, and strategy played on a pool table using the cue ball, called the shooter ball, and just one striped ball, called the object ball. Only the corner pockets are used. The side pockets are blocked off by stuffing a roll of toilet paper in each. Pool cues are not used because pilots use their hands to "shoot" the shooter ball. Crud involves running the pool table in alternating teams frantically trying to grab the shooter ball and strike the object ball before it stops moving and sink it in one of the corner pockets.

———

Still, some of the changes I tried to implement at the squadron met with a bit of resistance because "the FNG is changing how things are done around here." Human beings are comfortable with status quo. We like what is traditional. I remember Colonel Woods pulling me into his office and saying, "Odie, I know you're getting some push back from some of the older pilots about what you're doing, but I see a lot of the morale and energy coming back. Keep doing what you're doing."

That was a Target Leader at work. He had his finger squarely on the pulse of the squadron and took the steps necessary to continue increasing our performance energy. What began as a series of little things grew into a big ball of synergy. With everybody working and flying together as one, the synergistic effect helped us go from the cellar to stellar within one year. When our squadron was retested in the ORI, we received the highest rating possible, "outstanding."

My flight commander wrote the following sentence in my first OPR (official performance report): "Lieutenant Espenship is directly responsible for the recent increase in the morale of the squadron." My OPR also noted that the uptick in squadron synergy and morale was directly responsible for the squadron attaining such a high rating for the ORI.

Synergy works not only in a fighter squadron but also in big corporations. During a break between sessions of several Target Leadership keynotes I was giving to Gulf Power Company, I was relating the above morale/synergy story to Bob Hobbs, safety and health manager at Gulf Power. He said, "Come over here, Odie; I want to show you something." We walked out to the parking lot, and he said, "Do you see all those service trucks parked there?" I looked out and saw a row of pristine white field service trucks perfectly lined up and backed neatly into each parking spot. The spacing between each vehicle was exact. It reminded me of air force Thunderbird jets perfectly lined up at an air show ready to fly.

I said, "Wow, Bob! Do you require them to do that?"

He grinned and said, "Nope, they did that on their own."

He went on to say that only a year prior, that specific group of employees was dead last in the entire company's "preventable vehicle accident" category. An accumulation of the little things, such as sideswiping mailboxes, running over curbs, and backing into stationary objects, kept them in last place until one driver got tired of the negative energy that came with always being at the bottom. He decided to take control, push the fight, and expend some energy. He stayed after work one evening and personally washed every one of those trucks. He then backed each truck into newly assigned parking spots, in numeric order, perfectly aligned. Night after night he did this. Others noticed and responded. They began helping. A sense of pride soon enveloped the entire group.

"And another thing," Bob said. "When they go to lunch together and park in the restaurant parking lot, they will find an open area where they can all park together, in numeric order, evenly spaced apart."

Within one year the group rocketed from worst to first, and it all started with one Gulf Power Company "fighter pilot" expending some energy, turning and burning, and winning! He turned antergy into synergy, and that is what Target Leadership is all about!

To list all the Target Leaders in my life who have inspired me like that would fill up about 50 chapters. Instead, I have decided to list some common energy traits I have sensed about them—in other words, the Target Leadership vibes that exuded from their pores and touched the soul like Aretha Franklin singing "Respect" at a frat party.

Similar to being given a call sign in a fighter squadron, I decided to give all those collective Target Leaders the call sign "CHI." CHI is a circulating life energy that, according to Chinese medicine, is the universal energy that permeates everything around us. Supposedly, CHI is present in all things, and it connects us to each other and to the earth itself. OK, I'm not going to ask you to sit cross-legged with your arms outstretched, fingers lightly touching, and hum "Ohmmmmm" before reading on. Just know that you give off an energy or a vibe to those around you. They pick up on it. They feel it.

All airmen must go through Escape and Evasion Survival School, which is an intensive program that teaches downed aviators techniques for evading a pursuing enemy. Basically, it is three days of jacked-up hide-and-seek in the woods with no food. While demonstrating how to use natural camouflage to better hide from an enemy who is really, really close, our survival instructor said something very interesting regarding giving off energy. He cautioned, "When hiding from an enemy who is coming near your location, control your breathing and do not stare at the enemy. Staring gives off an energy that says, 'Look: I'm hiding here.'" Ever get the feeling someone is staring at you? I do. Usually when I'm on stage.

Some of you may remember the F-16 fighter pilot Scott O'Grady, who was shot down in June 1995 while patrolling the no-fly zone in Bosnia. After ejecting into enemy territory, he used the evasion techniques very successfully when he eluded capture from the pursuing Serbian forces for almost six days before being rescued. His riveting story made national headlines.

People rarely, if ever, talk about their CHI, much less about what others perceive of their CHI—probably because it means discussing "feelings," and that's not a very dude-ish thing to do when operating in a dude-ish environment (I mean that generically, ladies, so please take it as it was intended).

Because CHI energy is more of a vibe or a feeling we get, it's not something we can taste or touch. You cannot look at someone's CHI as if you were looking at an engine to analyze why it isn't providing more power. Although CHI energy is not tangible, it can make tangible things better or worse, depending on the "feeling" each person has about whatever he or she is working on. For example, your team might complete a project on time (tangible), but it may be completed to minimum standards because no one was "feeling it" (intan-

> *People may forget what you say or what you look like, but they will always remember how you made them feel.*

gible). Conversely, when people feel a positive CHI energy (intangible) about completing a mundane job (tangible), the final result is usually well beyond mundane because everyone was "feeling it" (intangible).

As Target Leaders, we should be aware of and understand the powerful CHI that we have within us and how best to use it. Notice I said "be aware of and understand" your CHI. That means you do not have to discuss it with others unless you really want to. For example, when challenges arise, what affect does your CHI have on others? Do you pretend to fight but inside you are fleeing or looking for a way out? If you don't get your way, or if someone criticizes you, how do you typically respond? Are you defiant, tenacious, defensive, accepting, defeated, or aggressive? When everything is going well, what is your CHI response? Is it boastful, humble, arrogant, or gracious? The bottom line is that Target Leaders are aware of not only energy but also how best to manage it. The energy you bring to face your day, to address problems, and to work with your team should be constant, stable, and positive. When the dogfight gets hectic, chaotic, and stressful but your CHI is solid as a rock, people *feel* (intangible) they can count on you to guide them to the best solution (tangible).

Target Leaders display many high-level energy traits; however, I have chosen my favorite three. These energy traits are common not only in Target Leaders but also throughout all high-performing organizations. I used the acronym "CHI."

- **Competence**
- **Humility**
- **Integrity**

Employees will go the extra mile for you when they feel that type of CHI. They will respect you, believe in your leadership, and trust you to make the best decision(s). They'd hike Mount Everest in flip-flops for you. They'd tug on Superman's cape for you. If you asked them to jump, on their way up, they'd be asking, "How high?"

Competence CHI is something that develops over time. Competence does not brag about how good it is at doing certain tasks. Competence CHI just does it, and others notice. Remember that CHI is not what you say about yourself; it's what others perceive about you. Don't tell me how competent you are—just show me.

Many fighter pilots like to boast about how competent they are at dropping bombs and shooting the gun. To measure our competence at these skills, the air force has controlled gunnery ranges. Every bomb that is dropped and every bullet that is shot is measured for accuracy, and the scores are relayed back to the squadron for all to see. To make things interesting, there's a standard monetary bet: "Quarter a bomb, nickel a hole." That means that for every bomb you drop better than me, I have to pay you a quarter. Bullets work the same way. For every bullet I shoot through the acoustic scoring target better than you, you have to pay me a nickel. We are not talking about a lot of money here, but in any competitive environment, competence matters! Losing a nickel to a competitor is like, well, losing! Competence does not like to lose even a nickel.

I'll never forget a lesson I got learned one day from Mr. Competence. His name was Colonel "Bubba" Jenny, a meek, mild-mannered A-10 fighter pilot who was visiting our squadron from headquarters. I was chosen by Colonel Woods to be his flight leader for the week he was visiting. I was told to fly "nondemanding sorties" with Bubba as my wingman. He was the quiet type, smiled a lot, and exuded a very warm "happy to be here" vibe. I thought Bubba was the perfect call sign for him.

Even though Bubba was a colonel and outranked me, I was the flight leader, so I was responsible for planning the mission and giving the prejob briefing. He was my wingman, and although I showed respect for his rank, I was in charge of what we would be doing. I decided to take Bubba to the controlled gunnery range and do some level bombing. With the standard bet of a quarter a bomb, I figured I would win some of his money. At that time, the A-10 did not have a magic computing bombsight, so we bombed using manual pilot skill and technique. Level bombing is very difficult to do accurately without the aid of computers; however, I was pretty competent at it—or so I thought.

Bubba beat me like a rented mule that day on the gunnery range. As he was taking my money during our debriefing session, he looked at me with a grin and said, "Odie, beware of the quiet ones."

I asked how he did so well with the level bombing. I wanted to know his techniques. He said, "Well, I use the TLAR method" (pronounced tee-lar). Hmmm, I thought. Maybe this is some kind of new level-bombing procedure that I was unaware of.

Then Bubba said with a grin, "TLAR: that looks about right."

Competence CHI exudes an energy that whispers, "I am capable,

Competence lets the work do the talking.

talented, proficient, and adept in my field of work. The job will be completed to the highest standards." Competence understands the weak areas and guards against the temptation to pretend they do not exist. Competence is neither boastful nor arrogant. Companies and people alike overwhelm with loud promises and then underwhelm with lousy products. That makes our guard go up and our respect go down. CHI competence and respect cannot be taken; they can only be given.

Competence gives us the confidence to listen, decide, and then act. Competence consistently makes good decisions. In becoming competent leaders, learning to make good decisions often comes from making a few mistakes. As we learn, competence gives us the confidence to proceed on the best path.

Competence learns from mistakes. Humility transfers what is learned to others.

The "H" in CHI stands for humility. I believe *humility* is one of the most powerful CHI energy characteristics a Target Leader or a company can possess. A competent person learns so that he or she will not make the same mistake twice. Humility passes the lesson on so that *others* will not make the same mistake twice. Mistakes are embarrassing. Humility is liberating.

When companies or leaders attempt to insulate themselves from blunders, we have difficulty forgiving, trusting, and even liking them. How an entity applies the knowledge gained from a mistake demonstrates how humble it really is. When we see leadership make an honest effort to get at the truth and fix the problem, we trust them. As trust and respect build within the organization, they serve as an energy model for everyone.

Not only does humility transfer lessons learned to others but also its CHI energy compels Target Leaders to say, "I do not know everything, so please speak up if you see something going on that is not right."

Out of the air force at 28 years old, I was hired as a commercial airline pilot. My first revenue trip with passengers on board was in the Boeing 727. The captain was a seasoned 30-year airline veteran. I remember looking at him and thinking his pilot license was probably signed by Wilbur Wright. I was sure that if he wanted *my* opinion about anything, he would inform *me* exactly what *my* opinion was. He was very competent and in charge. I figured he knew everything. Yet through his humility CHI, my perception changed.

During his prejob briefing, I remember him saying clearly to me, "Jeff, you are fresh out of the Boeing 727 training. You know the systems of this airplane and the procedures as well as me. If you don't understand something I've said or something I am doing, ask immediately. I'll explain it again. If you still don't understand what is going on, we will stop what we are doing and figure it out. It's probably me who does not understand what is going on."

Here was a captain who instantly created a cockpit culture of open communication through his competence and humility CHI. The trip was four days long. I learned a lot from him because I felt comfortable asking a lot of questions. And because of his experience, he anticipated questions I should be asking.

My next trip was with another veteran captain. He introduced himself and congratulated me on being an FNG with the company. In his prejob briefing to me, he looked me square in the eyes and said, "Jeff, I run this ship exactly the way they taught you in training. If you see me doing something different from what the school taught you, speak up. I will listen. My skin is as thick as my skull." The trip was over before I knew it.

The next captain I flew with told me that he learned something new on every trip. He challenged me to "stay in the books" and keep up to speed on all the changes in policies and procedures. Captain after captain I flew with had the same humility CHI energy that screamed competence in the cockpit. This has helped me to become a better aviator and crew member.

To recap CHI:

- **C**ompetence learns from the mistake.
- **H**umility transfers the lesson.
- **I**ntegrity oversees the integration of the lesson and then monitors the performance of what was implemented.

Integrity is the most difficult CHI energy to have, and it is also the easiest to lose.

Target Leaders should ask, "Do the systems, methodologies, or policies I promote or ask others to follow have integrity? Do they actually work? Are the changes I promote for the good of the whole or ultimately for the good of me?" People are quick to see what is behind the curtain.

> *With integrity, nothing else matters. Without integrity, nothing else matters.*

People's perceptions are usually right on the money. People can see whether a new program or policy has integrity, works, or contributes to the greater good, and they will respond accordingly. Employees will wholeheartedly follow processes they perceive have integrity but will either pencil-whip or give lip service to those they feel do not.

I gave a presentation and held a CHI workshop for a Fortune 100 company. In the workshop, it came to light that their newly implemented "near-miss" reporting program had a substantial increase in the total number of reports than in the previous six months. On the surface, senior leadership was applauding this program as having "integrity." The increased near-miss reports seemed to indicate that the field employees were embracing the idea of reporting incidents. But were they really?

It came to light that although the program had good intent, it actually had very little integrity. Employees were submitting meaningless data in order to fulfill a quota set by management. This was an energy drain on everyone. The integrity of the program needed to be fixed or abandoned. Because the Target Leaders in the room made an honest effort to identify and implement programs that had integrity, they were able to openly discuss the issues. They came up with a better near-miss reporting system and a way to monitor its implementation. Open discussions are vital to helping organizations breathe integrity CHI back into broken processes. Resolving issues shows humility and reestablishes commitment and trust in future programs.

CHI energy is life. The better we understand our positive CHI energy traits, such as competence, humility, and integrity, the more synergy we create within ourselves and those around us. CHI energy gives us the courage to face at least one big fear today so we can be our own superhero tomorrow. Be proactive, take control, and push the fight to win.

ELEVEN

APPROACHABILITY: THE LAST DOMINO

T he law of gravity and the law of self-preservation are the two fundamental laws that govern plane and pilot. The law of gravity states that what goes up must come down. The law of self-preservation determines whether it is capable of going back up again.

If you disregard either of these fundamental laws, your words may be the last sound recorded on the aircraft's black box for posterity. Here are a few memorable last words. The copilot of one doomed airliner simply said "Ma, I love you" before impact. Another copilot decided to lash out at the captain, who got them in the predicament in the first place: "See! I told you!" Another copilot stated matter-of-factly, "We're gonna crash, Larry." To which Larry responded, "I know it!" Retired Delta captain and Vietnam-era fighter pilot Bill Jacobs told me of watching a friend's jet hit a ridgeline as they were making a bombing run down the Ho Chi Min Trail. Bill said that just before impact, his buddy squeezed the mic button and in a calm voice said, "Well, shit!"

Edward J. Smith, captain of the RMS *Titanic*, in an interview just prior to his fateful voyage, stated, "I have never been in an accident of any sort worth speaking about . . . I never saw a wreck and have never been wrecked, nor was I ever in any predicament that threatened to end in disaster of any sort."

What each of these ominous mini-monologues has in common is that it was spoken by a highly skilled, well-trained individual just like you and me. These people went to work that day and their families expected them to return home safely, but they did not.

Only afterward do we see all the leading indicators, like dominoes lining up ready to fall. All it takes is a slight nudge, a push, a change, a distraction, an assumption, an interruption and the first domino falls. Here they come, *clack*, *clack*, *clack*. Our ears are deaf to the noise, and our eyes are blind to the reactive chain of destruction coming at us until the last domino falls—*bang*! Lights out. This chapter is about interrupting the reactive chain of events to prevent the last domino from falling. Approachability is the answer. It's the courage to speak up and also the courage to listen. Many accidents have been avoided and prevented when someone had a missing piece of information and stood his or her ground long enough for others to pause and listen.

> *Approachability is like the canary in a coal mine. Listen to it sing. Your life depends on it.*

Approachability is a two-way street. Singing out and listening to the song are the easy parts of approachability. When flying and I hear another pilot say, "Hey, Odie, don't fly into that cloud—it's got a lot of granite and a few mountain goats inside of it," that's easy. I'll gladly change direction to avoid being on the six o'clock news.

The hard part of approachability is paying attention to what is not so obvious or listening to what is not being said. We may brush aside or fail to pick up on many nonverbal cues that prove to be the final domino. Paying attention or responding to a vague statement, a rhetorical question, a shoulder shrug, or a quizzical look can be difficult. My brother gave me a quizzical look when I told him not to worry about pulling the propeller blade through. That look was saying something, but I failed to listen. He was the canary that stopped singing. He did not sing out loudly enough with words, and I was the miner who failed to listen. This is the part of approachability that is so difficult.

To illustrate how challenging approachability is, I want to step through three commercial airline accidents. My purpose is not to judge the players or throw blame. My hope is to take what they gave us and raise our awareness for when the canary stops singing at our place of work.

- Air Florida flight 90 crashed into the icy Potomac River, January 1982 (74 fatalities).
- Comair flight 5191 departed from the wrong runway in Lexington, Kentucky, August 2006 (49 fatalities).
- Pan Am and KLM 747s crashed on the island of Tenerife, leading to the worst aviation accident in history (583 fatalities).

Let's look at the final dominoes of Air Florida flight 90. Just as the working crew begins the takeoff roll:

Cockpit voice recorder transcripts

COPILOT: God, look at that thing. That don't seem right, does it? Uh, that's not right [referring to engine gauges].
CAPTAIN: Yes, it is; there's 80 [referring to airspeed].
COPILOT: Naw, I don't think that's right. Uhhh, maybe it is.
CAPTAIN: 120 [referring to accelerating airspeed].
COPILOT: I don't know.

With the plane now barely airborne, we can hear the continuous sound of the "stick shaker," which warns pilots of an impending stall, until impact.

CAPTAIN: Stalling! We're falling!
COPILOT: Larry! We're going down, Larry!
CAPTAIN: I know it!

When employees in the field are unsure of what they are seeing or experiencing, they may not be able to articulate exactly what they can or cannot see. It is difficult to clearly explain a bad feeling you are having, especially to a supervisor. Approachability in the workplace may look or sound something like:

"Hey, this doesn't seem right, does it?"

or

"This light is . . . uhh . . . the light is usually off—the power is off, right?"

or

"These . . . uhh . . . these . . . uhh . . . are these—yeah, these are the right pressure fittings for this, yeah."

or

Insert your own unsure/vague workplace example here.

Approachability means *be on the lookout* for the rhetorical question, the vague statement, or the unsure utterance. It might be your final domino.

The second mishap comes from the final moments of Comair flight 5191. Three experienced pilots in the cockpit departed from the wrong runway in Lexington, Kentucky, August 2006, resulting in 49 fatalities.

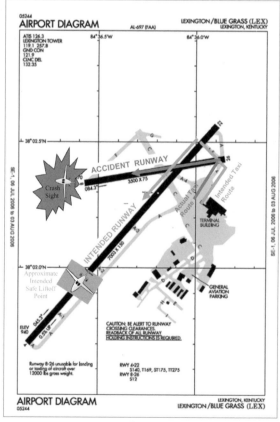

Kentucky Airport diagram.

It is early morning and still dark out as the captain taxis the airplane to depart on runway 22 (see airport diagram). Instead, he mistakenly turns onto runway 26, a runway that is too short for the required takeoff roll. How could this happen to a highly experienced captain, to a normally alert copilot sitting next to him, and to another pilot sitting in the jump seat and hitching a ride to work? Unfortunately, many human behavior errors allowed the dominoes to continue to fall. My purpose is not to dissect those errors. I wish to raise our awareness of how difficult approachability is because it does not always come from a person. The job itself might be trying to tell us something, yet we fail to listen. There are numerous non-verbal hints and clues that we fail to act on when working. It might be a part on a machine that is missing, a broken wire, misbehaving equipment, or malfunctioning lights.

The Comair flight 5191 crew was no different. The runway edge lights on runway 26 were off deliberately because it was not the active runway, but the pilots failed to pay heed to this non-verbal clue. Attempting to takeoff on a runway without the runway edge lights is a violation FAA regulation (Part 121) for night operations. The fact that the lights should have been on served as the final domino warning the pilots that they might be on the incorrect shorter runway.

As they began their takeoff roll down the unlit runway, approximately 12 seconds into the work, the first officer said, "Is weird with no lights." To which the captain replied, "Yeah." Nothing else was heard until 15 seconds later when the captain made an exclamatory "Whoa!" as the end of the short runway appeared. He attempted to get airborne and fly, but he did not have enough airspeed to sustain flight. Energy is life. The sounds of the crash followed shortly thereafter.

As we read this, we might be thinking, "How could they be so stupid?" If three highly skilled, well-trained pilots like that could make an approachability error like that on the job like that, so can I, and so can you. Approachability is not always black and white.

Let's look again at situational awareness (SA), the measuring stick for our perception of reality versus actual reality. Taxiing an airplane onto the correct runway can be perceived as a low-risk event. Pilots always get it right. This perception lured all three crewmembers into a trap; they failed to verify the correct runway. They believed they were on the right one.

Beliefs are extremely powerful drivers of humans' emotions to act or not to act. The lack of runway lights was trying to speak up, but all three pilots failed to listen because they *believed* they were on the correct runway. There was construction going on at the Lexington airport at the time. Did the pilots rationalize that the runway lights were off for that reason? We will never know. We do know they continued the takeoff, wanting to maintain their perception of reality as being real. In these cases, we want to be right, but if the job is hinting that something isn't right, listen to the clues. Hearing someone make the statement "Is weird with no lights" might be your last domino if you fail to act.

The final accident is perhaps the saddest. It stands today as the worst aviation accident in history. Five hundred and eighty-three people lost their lives when two 747 jumbo jets collided on a fog-enshrouded runway at Tenerife Island in March 1977. Poor approachability was the culprit in allowing the last domino to fall.

Dominoes can line up and begin falling when we are adapting to a required change, usually involving one or a combination of the place, the plan, or the people. Being flexible to change is necessary. Trees that are rigid and unbending snap easily when the wind blows too hard. Being able to bend and flex when changing pressures come our way is tantamount to our survival. However, during winds of change, a heightened sense of awareness and approachability is a key component of preventing the dominoes from falling.

On this fateful day, a Pan Am 747 jumbo jet and a KLM 747 jumbo jet were en route to their destination, the Las Palmas Airport (also called Gran Canaria Airport). A terrorist bomb had exploded there, which caused a change in not only the plan but also the place. These two planes, along with many other commercial airliners, had to be flexible. They diverted and landed in Tenerife, a much smaller airport located in the Canary Islands off the west coast of Africa. The new plan called for everyone to wait there until the Las Palmas Airport reopened.

At this point, the taxiway at the tiny Tenerife Airport was full of parked commercial airplanes. This was one in a series of dominoes quietly lining up. After several hours of waiting, word finally came that the Las Palmas Airport had reopened. With only one takeoff runway and airplanes clogging the taxiway, at Tenerife the planes had to follow a procedure known as a backtaxi. Airplanes use the runway as a taxiway to backtaxi to the very end, turn around, and then use the full length of the runway for takeoff. This was another domino lining up.

The air traffic control tower is responsible for choreographing this procedure as well as issuing takeoff clearances at the airport. A number of planes successfully took off in this fashion at Tenerife. As the slow process continued, a heavy fog descended over the airport. Fog poses a significant challenge to pilots but is not an insurmountable one. It reduces visibility, which increases risk. To operate safely in fog, everyone must work at a slower pace, maintain a heightened level of awareness and vigilance, and communicate location information more than when visibility is clear. This was another domino lining up.

The airplanes continued to cautiously taxi down the runway, turn around completely, and take off, staying in close communication with the tower at all times. Finally, their turn came. The KLM 747 had traversed the length of the runway and then turned around in preparation for take-off. Per instructions from ground control, the Pan Am 747 was taxiing immediately and directly behind the KLM.

The Pan Am aircraft was instructed to travel down the runway and then exit the runway by taking the third turn on the left to leave the runway clear for the KLM plane to take off. KLM was instructed to hold until Pan Am called "clear of the runway." Because of the fog, the Pan Am pilots, Captain Victor Grubbs and his copilot, Bob Bragg, were having difficulty locating the third exit. Captain Grubbs was taxing the airplane and Bragg was talking on the radio to the tower while trying to identify the correct taxiway.

TOWER: Affirmative, taxi into the runway and . . . ah . . . leave the runway third, third to your left.
PAN AM: Third to the left, OK.

Pan Am Captain Grubbs thought he heard "third one to your left" and questioned Bragg if the tower meant "first one to your left." Bragg said, "I'll ask him again." More dominoes were lining up as Pan Am was slow to exit the runway.

By now, at the very end of the runway was the KLM airplane, poised for takeoff. The senior KLM captain was anxious to get back on schedule.

There was some confusion in his cockpit about whether they had received proper clearance to take off. As the captain advanced the throttles, the copilot quickly advised him that air traffic control clearance for takeoff had not yet been given.

The KLM captain indicated that he knew he had not received clearance and told the copilot to ask for it. The copilot radioed the tower that they were ready for takeoff and waiting for air traffic control clearance, which is given with in-flight routing and direction details. The KLM pilot received instructions that specified the route they were to follow after takeoff.

If we listen to the recording of the air traffic controller's interaction with the pilot, it becomes clear that the instructions they were given included the word "takeoff" but did not actually provide takeoff clearance. The copilot read the flight clearance information back to the tower and said they were "now at takeoff." The captain interrupted the copilot's read-back with the comment "We're going." To clarify, the controller immediately added, "Stand by for takeoff; I will call you," clarifying that KLM did not have clearance for takeoff.

A simultaneous call from the Pan Am crew caused mutual interference on the radio frequency, resulting in a three-second-long whistling sound (heterodyne) in the KLM cockpit. This sound interfered with the KLM crew's ability to hear the controller's last statement. The Pan Am crew was indicating they were still taxiing down the runway, but because of the radio interference, this would have been difficult for the KLM crew to hear. A few more dominoes lining up, ready to fall.

My video producer and partner at OdieVision, Audie Osborn, and I personally interviewed the Pan Am copilot, Bob Bragg. I asked him about this fateful radio call that had been blocked by interference. Bob said he heard KLM announcing "now at takeoff" and "we're going," so he immediately pressed his microphone button to protest KLM's decision to take off by saying, "Pan Am is still on the runway. Do not take off!" The control tower was protesting as well. These two radio transmissions obstructed each other, causing the interference on the KLM radio. By now, the fog was so thick that neither plane could see the other and neither could be seen from the control tower. This was a significant problem since this smaller airport was not equipped with ground radar. As a result, both the actual location and the relative location of the two aircraft were unknown to all involved. The dominoes began falling as the KLM captain assumed that Pan Am was clear of the runway.

The KLM captain started the takeoff roll again just as the tower instructed the Pan Am crew to report when they were clear of the runway, which they acknowledged they would do. The KLM flight engineer again expressed concern about the Pan Am aircraft not being clear of the runway. His concerns were dismissed by the captain. The next few minutes of radio transmission show the final domino crashing on the concrete runway.

Zulu times recorded by the black box in hours and minutes (1706) and in seconds down to the hundredth decimal (25.47):

1706:25.47 **AIR TRAFFIC CONTROLLER:** Ah . . . Papa Alpha 1736, report runway clear. ["Papa Alpha" is phonetic spelling of "PA," which refers to Pan Am's call sign.]

1706:25.59 **PAN AM PILOT BRAGG:** OK, we'll report when we're clear.

1706:31.69 **AIR TRAFFIC CONTROLLER:** Thank you.

At the far end of the runway, the KLM captain advances the throttles for takeoff.

1706:32.43 **KLM ENGINEER:** Is he not clear, then?

1706:34.10 **KLM CAPTAIN:** What do you say?

1706:34.70 **KLM ENGINEER:** Is he not clear, that Pan American?

1706:35.70 **KLM Captain:** Oh, yes! [emphatically]

Being in a hurry to take off in a heavy fog and misunderstanding the control tower led to a degradation in approachability of the KLM captain. Pan Am copilot Bragg saw the massive KLM 747 emerging from the fog and heading straight toward them. The Pan Am cockpit microphone recorded the shock in Bob Bragg's voice, "There he is . . . look at him! Goddamn, that son of a bitch is coming! Get off! GET OFF!"

In the same moment the KLM captain saw the Pan Am jet loom out of the fog directly in front. With no time to stop, he yelled an expletive, "OH!" as he tried to fly over the top of the Pan Am 747. The KLM captain pulled back on the control yoke so aggressively that the tail section of his airplane struck the runway and left deep craters in the reinforced concrete. The KLM jet failed to have sufficient airspeed to gain enough altitude. Energy is life. Its belly and landing gear tore into the top of the Pan Am 747.

As Pan Am copilot Bragg was yelling "GET OFF! GET OFF THE RUNWAY!" Captain Grubbs pushed all four throttles to maximum power and headed toward the grass. Just prior to impact, Bragg remembered seeing the red rotating beacon flashing underneath the belly of the KLM 747. He instinctively ducked and waited for the impact. He was surprised to feel only a slight bump—"that was it." Thinking KLM must have cleared the top of his plane with minimal damage, Bragg sat back up. "The first thing I noticed was all the windows in the cockpit were gone," he recounts. "I looked directly behind me and where the upstairs lounge had been; we had 28 passengers up there. The lounge and the people were missing— gone, GONE! It was as if someone took a big knife and shaved the entire top of the airplane off. I could see all the way back to the tail. That's when I realized what damage he had done."

There were two Pan Am mechanics riding in the jump seats right behind the pilots. Bob recounted to me that the jump seats were also completely gone, as if they vanished into thin air. He later found out that they were hanging upside down underneath the cockpit. Miraculously, the mechanics survived. Upside down, they released their seat belts and were dropped on their heads. They scurried to safety. It reminded me of landing in the sand dunes at Myrtle Beach and flipping upside down and then scampering out to safety.

By now, Bragg said the noise was deafening. The four massive engines of the Pan Am 747 were still running. They tried shutting them off using the cutoff switches, but all controls to the engines were rendered inoperative by the collision. The fire handles for the engines were located on the overhead instrument panel. It, too, was missing. Temporal distortion took over. Bragg remembers standing up and jumping over the side. He landed in soft grass, completely uninjured.

Captain Victor Grubbs jumped through the area where the cockpit door used to be. It was his habit to exit there, only this time he fell into the cabin section below and suffered significant burns. He wound up in the forward cargo as he fell through the lower floor.

By now, Bragg was standing in front of the massive airplane that was engulfed in flames. He saw passengers standing on the left wing. He motioned and yelled for them to "JUMP OFF!" They complied immediately as they poured off the leading edge of the wing like ants. Through the mayhem,

Bragg told me that he recalled seeing a man holding a woman by her ankles. "He was in dead run dragging that lady by her feet," he said. Puzzled, he later found out why. The lady was the man's wife. When Bragg motioned for everyone to jump off the wing, she was the first to jump. Consequently, everyone landed on top of her, which broke her back and both her legs. The man was dragging her to safety. To this day, Bragg is haunted by that memory but is consoled knowing at least they survived.

—⁂—

Audie and I spent a fascinating few days with Bragg at his home in Virginia that culminated in a 16-minute safety leadership training DVD called Leading Indicators: The Tenerife Tragedy.

Produced by OdieVision LLC, the movie contains many excerpts from Bragg as he recounts what happened and why. The DVD is perfect for generating Target Leader discussion on the following topics:

1. *Unexpected changes in work activity.*
2. *Failure to recognize hazards.*
3. *Approachability and failure to listen.*

—⁂—

In no way should we lay all blame at the feet of the KLM captain. Although KLM accepted responsibility, many contributing factors started the dominoes falling.

Approachability in the KLM cockpit would have certainly prevented the final domino from hitting the ground. The lessons laid the foundation for cockpit resource management (CRM), a safety and awareness process for airline pilots. CRM is a method designed to optimize team performance by reducing the effect of human error through optimal use of

If you see something, say something, do something.

people, technology, and processes. This systems-based approach to safety focuses on emphasizing standard operating procedures, understanding the nature of errors, and, most important of all, developing an environment that does not punish honest mistakes.

Three primary error management techniques were learned:

- Error mitigation—An error was committed, but because it was discovered, highly trained personnel were able to mitigate its effects.
- Error trapping—An error was committed, but vital cross-checking procedures were followed, and the error was caught before it bore consequences.
- Error avoidance—This is the "do something" part of "if you see something, say something, do something." The error was prevented by alert and experienced personnel.

Creating a culture of approachability encourages less experienced team members to speak up and even challenge their supervisors when they believe something is not correct. Supervisors are encouraged to stop the work and listen to their crew. Any misunderstandings in the cockpit, in the office, or in the field must be explained and understood by everyone before proceeding.

I cannot thank Bob Bragg enough for allowing Audie and me a few days of his time to share and learn. He is the embodiment of a Target Leader. His CHI energy exuded competence, humility, and integrity. He went on to a long and successful career with Pan Am as a Boeing 747 captain and instructor. He helped implement many of the CRM techniques and methodologies. We thank pioneers such as Captain Bragg who pass the lessons on. It is our responsibility to have the humility to not only learn from these lessons but also monitor the integrity of implementing whatever changes are derived from them.

Hindsight is 20/20, but having foresight is 20/20/20. That means every 20 minutes, take 20 seconds and look 20 feet around you. Approachability is taking the time to stop, listen, and gain new perspective. It might be the one time you prevent the final domino from slamming into the ground.

TWELVE

COMMUNICATION: CONVERSATION, NOT CONFRONTATION

W hile standing at the gate and waiting to board a flight to Hawaii, I overheard the following bit of miscommunication between two passengers who did not know each other.

The first passenger nodded and said, "Hah-wah-ya?" to the second passenger.

In response, the second passenger pointed to the sign above the gate and said, "I hope so. That's what the sign says."

I could see an invisible Microsoft hourglass pop up and slowly start spinning above the first passenger's head as his brain was trying to process the data from the second passenger's input. The second passenger saw the same spinning hourglass above the first passenger's head. Sensing this vibe of confusion, the second passenger was prompted to act. He stepped out of line and walked over to the ticket agent who was feverishly working the boarding process. "Excuse me," he interrupted, "but this flight *is* going to Hawaii, right?"

The gate agent stopped what she was doing, looked up, and said, "Yes, Sir, it is." She started back to work and then stopped. I saw a Microsoft hourglass start spinning above her head as she contemplated, What may have caused the passenger to ask that question? Did I communicate the wrong destination during my last public announcement? Now fully distracted from what she was originally doing, the gate agent walked over to the ticket counter, picked up the mic, and made another announcement confirming Hawaii as the final destination. By now the second passenger was back in line confirming to the first passenger that they were in fact at the correct gate going to Hawaii. To which the first passenger replied, "I know. I just asked how you were doing."

I live in an area of the country where the word "Hawaii" and the phrase "How are you" are pronounced nearly identically: "Hah-wah-ya." The second passenger erroneously assumed the first passenger was asking whether they were at the correct gate to Hawaii, when in fact the first passenger simply asked, "How are you?" (Hah-wah-ya?) This bit of miscommunication caused the Microsoft hourglass to pop up and start spinning above both of their heads. Acting on a faulty premise, the second passenger stepped out of line and interrupted a very busy gate agent, thus pulling her off task.

Many of you are master communicators and probably already know how to fix the above example of being misunderstood. I can already hear what you're thinking about the two passengers: unless he is attending a NASCAR race, the first passenger should learn to *eeeeenuunceeeate* better.

and

The second passenger should not be so quick to assume what is being said or asked. It is best to clarify information before acting on what may be a faulty premise and causing problems for everyone involved. Some problems are minor; some are deadly.

Do not communicate hoping to be understood. Communicate so that it is impossible to be misunderstood.

A tragic scenario for anyone is to be part of an accident that happened because we were misunderstood. Here is another example of miscommunication:

Supervisor: Why did you do that? What were you thinking?

Employee: I was doing exactly what you told me to do!

Supervisor: That is not what I told you to do!

Employee: Well, uh, I thought . . . uhhh . . . I guess I misunderstood what you told me to do.

Supervisor: How could you misunderstand my instructions? I even asked if you understood what I said and you nodded yes.

Employee: I nodded yes because I thought I understood.

The two are discussing who is most at fault for the misunderstanding mishap. They really should be discussing how the message one intended for the other was so vastly different from what was heard. Instead, their Adam and Eve Garden of Eden human DNA urges them to blame the other. This is a simple illustration of how a conversation can quickly escalate into a confrontation, either at home or at work. Sound familiar? To me, the simple answer to many misunderstandings lies in our different life experiences. For example, when I hear words, I subconsciously mix what I am hearing with my personal knowledge and experiences. A biased opinion forms in my head of what I believe is meant. With good intent, I act based on what may be a faulty premise. Hopefully, I get it right. In the cockpit of life, acting on hope is not good. When things matter, Target Leaders consider the following key points when communicating:

- Ask specific follow-up questions about what was just discussed. Asking "Do you understand?" is not a good follow-up question. It's almost guaranteed someone will nod his or her head yes because in that person's mind, he or she really does understand. Push the fight when communicating. Be proactive to learn more about what is being said.

- Resist the urge to be an interruptive listener, either verbally or mentally. Interrupting indicates that your brain is going on autopilot and you are assuming what someone is trying to say or what someone intends to say. Hear the person out. You might be surprised at what comes out of his or her mouth.

- Don't roll your eyes or huff out loud at anyone when trying to communicate. It sends an unintentional message of "Are you stupid?" Don't get frustrated. Remember that you might be the one who misunderstands. Be thankful you're finding out now how little someone really understands about the job instead of realizing it when he or she is halfway through.

Accidents have happened because the job was too complex for the worker but the worker felt capable of handling it. Had the right questions been asked beforehand instead of "Do you understand?" it would have become apparent that the worker needed more supervision and training before working solo.

Hear with your ears but listen with your mind.

As a Target Leader, asking the right questions is vital to avoiding or clearing up misunderstandings. Never assume. You might act on faulty data that might be deadly data. Unfortunately, we fail to recognize when communication is done well. It gets our attention only when it appears in an after-action report. Therefore, in an effort to recognize excellent communication between customer and company, I want to highlight the following conversation I recently had with a Comcast customer service representative (I'm not sure what this person's real title was, but this is the title I'm assigning for this book). She very effectively used a shortened version of an active listening protocol that I will discuss in more detail later in this chapter. This is a generalization of what transpired between us:

COMCAST CUSTOMER SERVICE REPRESENTATIVE (CCSR): "Thank you for calling Comcast. May I help you?" (OK, I can't remember her exact greeting.)

ME: I have several telephone lines, and I need to discontinue the use of one of them. I no longer need it.

CCSR: If I heard you correctly, Mr. Espenship, you would like to discontinue the use of one of your telephone lines because you no longer need it; is that correct?

ME: That is correct.

CCSR: OK, I can understand why you would want to discontinue the use of a telephone line that you no longer need. May I get the number of the telephone line that you no longer need?

ME: Yes. The number is (404) 353-5555.

CCSR: I understand that the number you wish to disconnect is (404) 353-5555.

ME: That is correct.

The conversation between us continued in the above manner until we hung up. When business matters, communicating like that leaves little opportunity for error, assuming, or disconnecting the wrong business telephone number. Comcast did not pay me for the plug, but I am glad to give credit to the company for training its employees to use a highly reliable communication model. The next time you speak to someone in a customer service department, pay attention to how well the representative "listens to understand" what you need. If he or she does a good job, you will recognize it right away, as I did with Comcast. Who knows—you might pick up a few more good listening techniques. On the flip side, you will recognize when the rep doesn't do well listening to you. When that's the case, you will get to practice good listening skills in reverse. Ask probing questions to make sure you are heard correctly. "Will you please repeat back what you understood I need?" works perfectly.

How many accidents did not happen because a Target Leader took the time to thoroughly communicate? How many refinery explosions, oil rig fires, or construction accidents were avoided because someone listened to every worker's perception regarding what should be done and how best to do it? How many airline crashes were avoided because the pilots and the controllers used proper communication hear-back/read-back techniques and did not assume what the other meant? The short answer to these questions is simple: *all of them.*

When we are misunderstood, the communication can easily go from a conversation to a confrontation. When this happens, feelings are hurt and people become resentful, even spiteful. Performance goes down, and anger goes up. The mandibles come out, and the verbal jabs come in. But wait! While going through relationship-communication counseling, I learned a communication tool that can be employed by both sides. Over the years of using it, I have taken the liberty of modifying it for Target Leaders. I call it the active listening protocol (ALP), and I use it to effectively revert verbal confrontation to conversation. It works only if both sides can agree to this very simple premise: the ALP helps both parties mutually *understand* each other's position and point of view by eliminating faulty premises and assumptions. After utilizing the ALP, participants may or may not agree on the opinions, beliefs, or outlook of the opposing side, but there will be no misunderstanding of each other's position.

Even though the sides may not agree with each other, any decision to act made afterward will be done with the correct information. Having correct information means a Target Leader can pursue the *best* course of action and not a course of action based on assumptions. You might be a parent, a community leader, or a supervisor who has to make a difficult or controversial decision. Once you make your decision to act, the opposing party might not like the decision you've made, but there is a much greater chance that he or she will support you in your decision because you took the time to listen and understand his or her views.

Now, before I share how to employ the ALP, I have to be honest. When I was first learning how to do it, I thought the whole thing was, well, a bit too touchy-feely and time-consuming for me. You might feel the same way I did before trying it out. However, my desire for being understood and understanding others overcame my biases and my busy schedule. The older I get, the more aware I am of the impact my decisions have on the safety of others. This is especially true when sitting at the controls of a Boeing 777 and flying 280 people halfway around the world. Decisions in that environment must be as close to operationally perfect as possible.

People just want to be heard.

After you give it a bit of practice, the ALP works—it really works—but you have to have the courage and willingness to try it. I decided to try it out on my 16-year-old daughter when she came home from school one day and announced that she wanted a tattoo. Now, I have nothing against tattoos! However, a 16-year-old girl in high school who wants a tattoo of a frog licking a mushroom with her boyfriend's name written inside a skull and crossbones directly underneath is *not* going to happen! OK, that's actually not the tattoo she had in mind, but it's what I assumed she wanted. This became the faulty premise I acted upon. I drew on my own opinions about teenagers:

- They have poor taste in tattoo art.
- They make hasty choices and then later regret those choices.

So without listening to her, I made my decision about her getting a tattoo: "NO!" Consequently, our conversation quickly degraded into a confrontation. She had her hand on her hip and her head cocked a little sideways (you know how they do), with a look that said, "You just don't understand, Dad!" I sensed an energy from her that exuded, "Well, I'm going to get it anyway and put it in a place where you can't see it."

It was right then that I thought, All right, I'll do this ALP thing and see whether it really works. I softened my face, lowered my tone, and asked her to please sit down. I expressed my willingness to not only hear what she had to say but also *understand* where she was coming from. In return, I wanted her to hear me out and *understand* where I was coming from. I told her I wanted to try a listening protocol that, if done correctly, would leave zero doubt about understanding each other. She stared at me as if my body had been taken over by aliens. She said, "I don't know who you are or what you have done with my dad, but I like you a lot better." And with that backhanded compliment, we both put our emotions on the shelf and began the ALP.

Step	Key Points	Description
1	Know the process	Before beginning, both parties must understand the methodology and agree to the protocol before proceeding. If either person is too angry, emotional, or heated to start, it is best to wait and cool down a bit before beginning. Both parties will decide who will speak first and who will listen first. Each will have a turn because the roles will swap after the first speaker is completely finished.
2	Speaking and listening	After deciding who speaks first and who listens first, you begin. As the speaker begins to speak, the listener must make eye contact with the speaker. The listener's body language must be attentive and focused. The listener must not roll his or her eyes, make facial gestures, or interrupt. The listener must remember what is being said, as he or she will need that information for the next step.

continued on page 126

Step	Key Points	Description
3	"What I heard you say was . . ."	Once the speaker has clearly finished talking, the listener states, "What I heard you say was . . ." and repeats the information exactly as he or she understood it. It is important that the listener does not add his or her own spin, thoughts, or assumptions to what was said. The listener merely echoes the message. After this step, move on to step 4 by asking, "Did I get it right?"
4	"Did I get it right?"	When the listener asks, "Did I get it right?" much of the time, the listener will have misunderstood some or all of what the speaker was trying to say. Do not get discouraged by this because this is the step that proves how easily we can misunderstand what was just said. Therefore, this step is vital to making sure the information was echoed correctly. Repeat steps 3 and 4 until the speaker is completely satisfied that the listener has repeated the information correctly. Only when the speaker says to the listener "Yes, you got it right" can the parties move on to step 5.
5	"Is there more?"	Once the speaker confirms that he or she has been heard correctly, the listener asks, "Is there more?" In this step, the listener communicates that he or she wants to understand "more" if there is more. When the speaker has said his or her piece and the listener has echoed it to the speaker's satisfaction, the speaker says, "No, there is no more." Now, the speaker has been heard and understood. Swap roles.
6	Taking turns	The parties change roles and start at the top. Follow the same process to ensure there are no misunderstandings.

Back to my 16-year-old daughter and the giant body tattoo I assume she wants. Here's how the ALP played out for us that day the aliens took over my body. She spoke first; I listened. She was very articulate, and I did my best to listen and really hear what she was saying. Wow, I thought, she sure has a lot to say! We had

Discussion is an exchange of knowledge; an argument is an exchange of ignorance.

—Robert Quillen

to keep repeating steps 3 and 4. Sometimes I would incorrectly repeat what she just said. Sometimes I would interject my personal opinion or omit something altogether. She took delight in correcting me. Eventually, though, I finally got it all right. When we moved on to step 5 and I asked her, "Is there more?" her face was completely radiant. Her demeanor was relaxed. She had more to say, and she knew I was committed to listening and getting it right. Her attitude was open as she spoke with candor. I listened intently. My eyes focused on her face, and my ears captured her words. This conversation turned into something much more than a discussion about her taste in tattoos. For the first time, I was really listening to her perceptions and thoughts about me, not only as a dad but also as a person. This really helped us both.

Then we swapped roles, and it was my turn to speak and her turn to listen. Her energy was open and receptive. Her attitude was that she wanted to be a better listener to me than I was to her. After she heard where I was coming from on the whole tattoo thing, the solution she proposed was brilliant. I'll never forget it. She decided to put a drawing of the tattoo she wanted on the refrigerator. If she still liked it six weeks later, then we would have another *conversation* about her getting that tattoo. Deep down, I knew her mind changed as the wind blew. She posted the tattoo drawing she made on the refrigerator. Actually, what she drew did not look bad at all. It was very tasteful, unlike the images I had in my head from preconceived ideas.

Two weeks went by and she came into my office holding another picture she had drawn. Smiling, she said, "Hey, Dad, what do you think about this for a tattoo?" She liked this drawing better. Truthfully, so did I. She wanted to swap it with the one on the refrigerator. Now, it would be easy for me to gloat and say, "Changed your mind so soon?" But that is counterproductive and not being a Target Leader. Instead, I complimented her on the new artwork. We agreed that she could remove the old picture from the refrigerator and replace it with the new one. We reset the clock for another six weeks.

Nine days later she had another version she liked "even better"! This process repeated for a few months until one day it fizzled out. She saw how easily she changed her mind about what she wanted. She finally did get a tattoo she wanted—but six years later! It's a small one on the back of her shoulder, written in script. It says, "Shine On You Crazy Diamond," a lyric by the great band Pink Floyd. To me, that lyric reveals much about who my daughter has become at this stage of her young adult life. She is my crazy jewel whose inner beauty, like a radiant cut diamond, shines on my life.

Relationships are about relating to each other and understanding where the other person is coming from. The ALP will help if you remember to keep your emotions in check. As I have continued to use the ALP technique, here are a few big mistakes I have made when using it:

- When the other person was speaking, I would interrupt, or maybe roll my eyes, or try to finish what he or she was trying to articulate.
- When repeating information, I would add my own thoughts, spin, or judgments based on my own experiences, not from what the other person was saying.
- When I repeated the information, I had the feeling that the other person must have thought I was agreeing with what he or she was saying when in fact I was not. I had to remind myself that I was simply echoing what he or she was saying, assuring him or her that I "got it right."
- I was not as patient or open-minded as I needed to be when the other person was speaking.
- Sometimes, it was upsetting for me when the other person *clearly* understood my point of view but did not like it. I had to struggle to remember that the ALP is about understanding each other and not necessarily agreeing with each other. I had to accept that.

Not all of your disagreements will turn out the way you want, but I do encourage you to try this technique. Ask your spouse, partner, workmate, or close friend to help you become a better communicator. Explain the rules, pick a knotty subject, and go for understanding each other's point of view. I think you will be surprised at:

- how much effort it takes to fully understand what the other person is trying to convey.
- how rewarding it is to truly understand another person's point of view.

- how little you really know about things you thought you understood.
- how good it feels to be understood by others in your life.
- how easy it is to misunderstand what is spoken—like "Hah-Wah-Ya."

Communication is about understanding. It is conversation, not confrontation.

DEADLY DISTRACTIONS

COPILOT: We did something to the altitude.
CAPTAIN: What?
COPILOT: We're still at 2,000 [feet], right?
CAPTAIN: Hey, what's happening here?
[sound of impact]

Those were the final words of the pilots of Eastern Airlines flight 401. Their day began like all the other days: routine. It was the evening of December 29, 1972, when the brand-new Eastern Airlines Lockheed L-1011 Whisperliner departed New York's JFK airport, headed for Miami. The flight ended with a crash into the Florida Everglades, resulting in 101 fatalities. How could a highly skilled, well-trained, competent cockpit crew of three, working together as a team, allow the airplane to fly itself into the Everglades?

It was a little thing, a tiny distraction that interrupted their normal routine. They became so focused on fixing it that the distraction turned deadly. They were trying to replace a lightbulb that had burned out on their forward instrument panel. This activity so channelized their attention they failed to monitor the status of the autopilot. They assumed it was holding the airplane at 2,000 feet when in fact it had inadvertently been disconnected. The airplane began slowly descending. Nobody recognized this fact until it was too late.

Think of the times something simple has distracted you, which then led you to become fully interrupted from what you were doing. Remember the gate agent who was briefly interrupted from her duty by the passenger who asked, "This flight *is* going to Hawaii, right?" Hypothetically, the distraction and subsequent interruption to make another PA to the passengers could have caused her to lose focus and fail to continue to properly enter the passenger boarding data into the computer. Incorrect passenger data can affect the weight and balance of the entire airplane, which can make it difficult—or, worse, impossible—for the pilots to handle.

An executive study by National Aerospace Laboratories (NLR) wrote an eye-opening executive study (http://www.skybrary.aero/bookshelf/books/1149.pdf) analyzing aircraft accidents related to weight and balance issues from 1997 to 2004. Many of these accidents happened as a result of "incorrect loading of the aircraft and the use of wrong takeoff weight for performance calculations." When we fail to stay focused on the task at hand, the distraction can become deadly.

Hindsight is always 20/20. It might be easy to judge high-performing teams for their errors in human behavior, but that is not how we as Target Leaders think. We learn the lessons from their errors with humility, knowing how easily it can happen to us if we fail to properly manage the interruptions we face during our normal duty. We add the lessons learned to our overall awareness. With every mishap, we keep filling our experience bucket so that changing burned-out lightbulbs in our future cockpits of life will never again become a deadly distraction. Let's go back in place and time, to that fateful night in south Florida, and learn.

On final approach into the Miami airport, the Eastern Airlines (EAL) flight 401 captain instructed his copilot to lower the landing gear. He said,

"Go ahead and throw 'em out" (taken from the cockpit voice recorder transcript).

The ill-fated EAL crew waited for the three green lights that indicated that all three landing gears were down and locked, but they failed to get the green light confirming that the nose gear was down. This meant one of two things: either the gear was not safely down and locked or the indicator lightbulb was burned out.

The captain decided to recycle the landing gear by saying, "I gotta . . . gotta raise it back up . . . Now I'm gonna try it down one more time." The light remained off. The copilot's voice was captured on the cockpit-area microphone as he asked the captain, "All right. Well, want me to tell 'em [referring to the traffic control tower] we'll take it around and circle around?"

The captain responded by making the following radio call to the control tower, "Ahh, tower, this is Eastern 401. It looks like we're gonna have to circle; we don't have a light on our nose gear yet." The pilots were given clearance to go into a holding pattern over the Florida Everglades and maintain an altitude of 2,000 feet until they figured things out. The dominoes were being lined up.

First, they had the burned-out bulb. Next, they could not use the horizon for a visual reference because it was dark outside. Sometimes when it is really dark out, looking out the front windscreen is like looking through a pot of two-day-old black coffee. You cannot see "the big picture." The Eastern pilots trusted the autopilot to hold them at the correct altitude while they worked on changing the lightbulb.

Another domino lined up when they could not get the bulb to fit correctly. The copilot thought maybe the assembly was not seated properly in the light panel fixture. He told the captain, "Uh, Bob, it might be the light. Could you jiggle the light?"

Forty seconds later, the copilot said to the captain, "We're up to 2,000 [feet]. You want me to fly it, Bob?" The captain answered with, "Yeah. Oh, I can't get it from here." I take this to mean the copilot was supposed to fly the airplane (via the autopilot) and the captain would work on fixing the bulb. At this point, the copilot's job was to fly the airplane; that's the big picture. The captain's job was to continue to work on the problem. Unfortunately, the light fixture the captain was working on was physically closer to the copilot. When the captain said to the copilot, "I can't get it from here," he was having difficulty reaching the assembly, so he instructed his copilot, "See if you can get the light out." This is a critical turn of events. Up to now, the copilot's primary job was to monitor the flight path of the airplane, but now the captain has assigned him the duty of helping with the bulb.

This was the nudge that began toppling the deadly line of dominoes. Both assumed that the autopilot would hold them steady at 2,000 feet. Neither the captain nor the copilot clearly reassigned work roles, and at that point the distractions became deadly. The copilot, being a helpful get-it-done kind of guy, became completely engrossed in fixing the light while the captain looked on. As the copilot struggled to remove and replace the fixture, the captain began leaning across the cockpit to help. Somehow, the autopilot accidentally disengaged. Investigators could not determine how it got switched off, but it most likely happened when either a hand inadvertently pushed the switch to the off position or a chest, knee, or other body part accidentally leaned forward into the control yoke with too much pressure. What we do know is that neither crew member noticed because he was so engrossed in trying to change "a goddamned 20-cent piece of light equipment," in the copilot's exasperated words.

With no visual cues outside the cockpit windows and the autopilot switched off, the airplane began a slow, imperceptible descent that the pilots failed to notice until it was too late. When the copilot finally checked the status of the airplane by looking at the primary flight instruments, what he saw on his altimeter shocked him. Instead of a reading of 2,000 feet, the altimeter showed 200 feet and slowly descending.

The cockpit-area microphone recorded their last words of puzzled bewilderment for posterity:

Copilot: We did something to the altitude.
Captain: What?
Copilot: We're still at 2,000, right?
Captain: Hey, what's happening here?
          [sound of impact]

By now, the Miami tower began to call, "Eastern . . . 401 . . . I've lost you, ah, on the radar there, your transponder. What's your altitude now?"

There was no response. A few minutes later, at 11:43 p.m., a transmission came in from a National Airline flight that happened to be in the area. "Miami tower, this is National 611. We just saw a big explosion; looks like it was out west. I don't know what it means, but I thought you should know."

This professionally trained, highly skilled team of Eastern pilots was no different from you or me. If it could happen to them, it can happen to us. Our duty is to learn from their mistake.

Crew resource management training and better error mitigation techniques no longer allow this type of communication between pilots when working a problem. We have specific procedures that we follow when handling distractions or working through difficulties. Changes were made to the autopilot system that immediately alert the pilots if it disengages for any reason. Changes were made that require air traffic controllers to immediately speak up and give corrective guidance to any airplane that strays off an assigned altitude or heading. Also, CRM has come a long way in teaching pilots how to recognize distractions and then methodically handle them. Not only are there operational distractions like EAL 401 but also there are mental distractions that can turn deadly. If we allow our minds to drift off task, we become mentally disengaged from our job. Therefore, every worker on a job must not only pay attention to his or her own responsibilities but also be aware of coworkers' job behavior and intervene if needed.

Years ago, while flying as a copilot on the Boeing 727, I found that my brain kept drifting off task. I was thinking about my brother, his family, and my parents and how much we all missed him. No doubt about it: this was a mental distraction. I kept missing checklist items, which the captain brought to my attention. I missed several radio calls, which the captain handled. The captain also noticed how often I was staring out the window with a 1,000-mile stare. Clearly, my mind was not keeping *the main thing the main thing*—flying the airplane.

What the captain did to fix the problem is a characteristic hallmark of a Target Leader. He stopped the work. Although it was my responsibility to handle all radio calls while he taxied the airplane, I had just missed another call from ground control. The captain picked up the mic and answered the call, and then he stopped the airplane in the middle of the busy taxiway.

This got my *full* attention. He looked at me and said, "Jeff, I have flown with you before, and you are a good pilot, but today, your mind is just not here. Relying on me to catch your mistakes degrades safety below the level I will tolerate."

As we sat still in the conga line of airplanes on the busy taxiway, he continued. "We have two choices. Either you can get on the radio and call the company and tell them I want another copilot or you can get your mind right. I'm sorry you are having problems concentrating. But when you come to work, you need to disengage your mind from those distractions and concentrate on what you are doing here. If you think you have problems now, wait until you miss an altitude or heading change because you are not focused. Your problem then becomes a problem for me, my family, and everyone else who may die as a result of your being distracted."

I am reminded of Paul Newman's 1967 movie *Cool Hand Luke.*

Boss Paul: You got your mind right, Luke?
LUKE: Yeah. I got it right. I got it right, boss.

Just like Cool Hand Luke, I made a decision to get my mind right, not only for that flight but also for all future flights. I promised the captain that I would stay focused for the rest of the trip. I also made a promise to myself to be on guard for mental distractions on future trips, within both myself and others. In more than 20 years of flying, I have kept the value of his "mental distraction" speech in my experience bucket. I have had to retrieve it a few times since and use it on myself and others as soon as I recognize the need. How many accidents have been avoided because of it? All of them.

What is most personal is most common. Here is a brief list of mental distraction indicators that you can watch out for.

Are you:

- Having trouble focusing while at work more than you used to?
- Realizing your workmates keep "covering" for you more than they normally would?
- Feeling unusually stressed or distracted?
- Going through a divorce or other relationship problem?
- Unable to sleep as well as you used to?

- Frustrated over trivial issues?
- Wondering whether your teenager is actually going to school while you are working?
- Dealing with a child or family member who has a substance abuse or medical problem?
- Dealing with a recent diagnosis of cancer or some other serious disease?
- In personal financial crisis?
- Working overtime or a second job just to make ends meet?
- Mourning the loss of a loved one?

I read a scientific study that said those who can easily and successfully focus on multiple tasks simultaneously represent less than 3% of the population. I know that I don't fall into that 3%, and in all likelihood, neither do you. The trouble is we fool ourselves into believing we are capable of handling multiple side jobs while still keeping an eye on the big picture, our main job.

When people tell me they are good at multitasking, I know they are good at doing many jobs poorly.

I went to the doctor's office recently because I had a cough and a raging sore throat. I had a speech to give in two days, and I needed help. The doctor asked what brought me to his office that day. I began to talk as he listened to my chest and looked down my throat and in my ears.

His cell phone buzzed, derailing his train of thought. He read the text message and said, "I don't know why they route prescription questions through this phone." He tapped in a brief reply and hit send. He sat down and faced the computer in the exam room. To increase efficiency, his practice had recently installed computer-based patient charts, so every exam room had a computer. With his back to me, he began clicking away, selecting different boxes on the screen to update my patient chart.

I asked, "So, what's wrong with me?"

"Bronchitis," he said.

Just then, the phone next to the computer rang and he answered it. It was the receptionist. She asked him to speak with a patient, who was on hold, regarding her prescribed dosage. "Put her through," he said.

The doctor spent the next five minutes trying to extract information from the patient on the phone about her ailment while clicking at a much slower pace on my computer chart. His mind was working double-time. He was not getting the answers he needed from the patient on the phone, so he minimized my chart on the computer and pulled up hers. He spent a few minutes reading, figured out what was missing in her patient chart, and finished up his call with her.

I was still sitting on the exam table, and the only words he had spoken to me thus far were "What brings you in today?" and "Bronchitis."

"So what do we do to fix it?" I asked.

"Shot of steroids will fix you right up" was his quick reply. He opened the door and said something to the nurse and left. The nurse came in, gave me a shot in the butt, said "There ya go," handed me some paperwork, and sent me on my way. Two days later my phone rang. It was the pharmacist informing me that my prescription was ready.

"What prescription?" I asked.

In a puzzled tone, the pharmacist answered, "Your antibiotic. It's been ready for two days."

I informed her that I wasn't aware that I required antibiotics. She immediately followed up with the doctor, who confirmed that I did, indeed, need to take antibiotics. So, right after breakfast, I headed to the pharmacy, picked up my prescription, and gulped down the first two pills to get started on my course of treatment.

Looking down, I read the information on the bottle: "Should not be taken within two hours of taking vitamins." Had the doctor been fully engaged, he would have mentioned the prescription, noticed on my chart that I take multivitamins every morning, and warned me about this drug interaction. As for my part, I should always read the small print before taking prescription medicine (mea culpa).

The doctor's new computer system allowed him to be more efficient at entering and tracking patient information and enabled him to send prescriptions directly to the pharmacist instead of writing them out by hand. I am not faulting the doctor's new system; I think it is a valuable improvement. In a five-minute time period he answered a text message, took the telephone call from the receptionist, pulled up another patient's chart, diagnosed my condition, updated my patient chart, and clicked the prescription button on the computer to send an order directly to the pharmacist. I was left out of the process and uninformed of the prescription.

Technology enables us to become more efficient and communicate faster, and it keeps our businesses competitive. As Target Leaders we must also be cognizant of the potential distraction these devices may cause, and we must set boundaries for their proper use. Employees may think they can do side jobs or personal work with this new, efficient technology but manage to do the additional tasks only poorly.

After the pharmacist called and told me my prescription had been waiting for two days, I decided to chat with my doctor about it. He quickly apologized and basically said, "I really don't know how that happened." I reached into my experience bucket and shared with him the "mental distraction" lesson the seasoned airline captain gave me many years ago when he stopped the airplane on the taxiway and "got my mind right." The doctor continued to listen as I explained to him how he failed to communicate with me during my office visit. I told him he allowed himself to use his new system's capabilities to multitask, which degraded his performance with me. At the end of our very cordial conversation, he understood the reason why so many of his patients were interrupting his already busy day and asking him to clarify information.

Doctors, like pilots, can get too comfortable handling routine work. We might fool ourselves into thinking we can handle all the extra distractions and still work quickly and efficiently. Day by day, we bite off a bit more, each time thinking our superior skills can handle the extra load until one day, one too many distractions leads to a fatal mistake.

On August 20, 2008, Spanair flight 5022 crashed while attempting to take off from Madrid-Barajas Airport. The investigation later revealed that the pilots attempted to take off without the flaps and slats set properly. These high-lift devices must be extended for all takeoffs; otherwise, the jet will simply run off the far end of the runway at a high rate of speed. Spanair flight 5022 served as the deadliest aviation accident in 2008 and also Spain's deadliest crash in 25 years: 154 people died and 18 survived. Attempting to take off without the flaps extended will *always* end in a crash at the far end of the runway. The number of survivors is up to God, luck, and physics—in that order.

This accident severely weakened Spanair's image with the public. If you mix a tarnished image with the financial difficulties that follow a major accident, the dominoes will start falling for any service company unless leadership acts decisively to rebuild public trust again. Unfortunately for Spanair, the final domino fell for the entire company in January 2012 when all operations ceased. I am not blaming the pilots for the demise of Spanair. We must remember that they were simply behaving, working, and responding within an entire system of company equipment, leadership, training, and supervision. That "system," created and maintained by the company, led the pilots of Spanair flight 5022 to make a mistake that accelerated the company's demise.

Rather than attempt to dissect the ills of Spanair the company, my purpose here is to raise awareness of deadly distractions that you and I may encounter. When the equipment blows up, it's you and me who die. When a company dies, it does so on paper. The employees may shed a few tears for the loss of their job, but when people cease to exist, families shed tears of grief for the loss of their loved ones. You and I are the ones who suffer loss, even death, if we allow "the system" in which we operate to make us complacent or distracted as we go about our daily routine.

We can learn from the Spanair pilots, people who were behaving in their routine *system*. Why did they attempt to take off without the flaps set? Commercial pilots know flaps are "kill me" items if not set properly for takeoff. The checklist instructs the pilots to check and recheck that the flaps are set at several intervals. If they still miss it, the takeoff warning horn is supposed to catch it. This warning is a last-chance lifesaving mechanical device that is built in to the airplane by the aircraft manufacturer. When the pilot pushes the throttles up for takeoff, the takeoff warning system does a final check of aircraft configuration to make sure systems such as the flaps, stabilizer trim, autobrakes, spoilers, etc., are positioned properly for takeoff. If not, the takeoff warning horn sounds really loud—BEEP-BEEP-BEEP—alerting the pilots to abort the takeoff and recheck the takeoff configuration. For the Spanair pilots, the takeoff warning system failed to work. It did not alert them that their flaps were not set properly for takeoff.

As part of the preflight checklist, pilots are supposed to check the takeoff warning system to make sure it is working properly. Had the Spanair pilots performed this preflight test, they would have known the system was inoperative. They would have been required to make a write-up in the aircraft logbook and have a mechanic repair the warning system.

- Were the Spanair pilots too complacent in proper checklist usage?
- How much emphasis did the company place on making sure this warning system worked?
- How often did company leadership go on observation flights to make sure all checklists were being adhered to correctly?
- Looking at the big picture, how often did the overall design of company operations contribute to task overload?
- How frequently do communications from the company to the cockpit interrupt the crew while doing their main job, flying the plane?
- How many times (leading indicator) have pilots attempted to take off without flaps but the warning horn "saved them"?

I asked friends of mine who work in safety management at major airlines, "Off the record, how many pilots at your airline have pushed the throttles up intending to take off but the takeoff warning horn sounded to alert them that the flaps were not set?" Their answers were shocking. A typical major air carrier does just under two million takeoffs per year. Out of all those departures, an average of five cockpit crew members attempted to take off without the flaps set. That means that five times per year, pilots overlooked the checklist in several areas regarding a critical safety "kill me" item. On the surface, five out of two million annual departures may not seem like a bad number when it comes to making mistakes, yet when it comes to relying on a mechanical device (takeoff warning horn) and hoping it will save you from certain death, that number should be *zero*. The only reason they did not end up on the six o'clock news was because the device worked as advertised and saved them.

The overwhelming reason that pilots (operators) miss critical items such as flaps is attempting to handle interruptions during already high workload times. These distractions cause task overload, and the crew must be proactive and slow the operation down.

For example, the before-takeoff checklist calls for the captain and copilot to read and verbally verify each item on the checklist. During high-workload times, pilots can ill afford to become complacent by parroting checklist items in a "you say *this* and I say *that*" manner. Normally, when one pilot verbally reads the checklist item "flaps," there is a canned response required by the other pilot—"Set 15 degrees"—but only after he or she verifies the condition. However, if the other pilot parrots back the canned answer, "Set 15 degrees," without actually verifying that the crucial component is set to 15 degrees, the distraction can become deadly. The other pilot hears the parroted response and in machine-gun staccato fashion continues reading the checklist under the false assumption that the critical item was verified. Many times, critical flight items such as flaps are repeated in different checklist areas. However, checklist complacency rears its ugly head when each pilot assumes the other has physically checked or ver-

> *So many times, failures are caused by the actions of sensible, rational people who were simply working to accomplish their goal in a manner they perceived to be safe, wise, and efficient.*

ified the items as they parrot the correct checklist response all the way to the runway. When they get cleared for takeoff and push the throttles up, the last domino is set, in hopes that the takeoff warning horn will operate properly, "BEEP, BEEP, BEEP," and save everyone from crashing at the far end of the runway. Are you willing to bet your life on it?

FOURTEEN

PRESSURE TO
PERFORM

The room full of utility linemen was thick with emotion. They had just lost one of their own to an electrical contact. Company management was taking questions from the bereaved group over the tragic loss of Mack, one of their most respected employees.

A burly lineman stood up, faced the manager, and blurted out, "Was the company putting pressure on him to hurry up and finish that job? Because you know you have been putting pressure on us for over two weeks to finish that job!"

Someone else chimed in with a similar pressure-to-hurry accusation and then another. The room was slowly turning into a cacophonous uproar of pent-up frustration and emotion. The company manager could hardly get a word in edgewise until a 30-year veteran lineman sitting in the front row stood up. He turned to face his union brotherhood sitting behind him. He held up his hands in a show of restraint. As the room quieted, I observed his resolute posture. I noticed he was missing his index finger.

As the room fell silent, he began to speak: "I was out there that morning Mack died. I had to shut off the power so we could retrieve his body. I had to identify his burned body for the coroner." His voice began to crack. He paused a moment to collect himself, turned toward the company manager, and continued: "I understand the pressure this company puts on us every day to finish our work."

The veteran lineman raised the nub of his missing index finger and pointed it directly at the manger and said, "When this company pushes me to finish a job before I'm ready, I PUSH BACK!" He made a pushing motion with both hands as if he were pushing back at the entire company.

The room was deadly quiet as he turned to face the crowd. He held up his hand with his missing finger and continued, "But when I push *me* to finish a job, I will splice live wire!" You could have heard a pin drop. Every worker in the room instantly understood that the internal pressure we put on ourselves to finish the job is far greater than perceived external pressures the company may put on us to complete work.

As an airline pilot, I took that hallowed piece of information and put it directly into my bucket of experience. Airlines run on a strict schedule, and our company's performance is measured by its on-time departures and arrivals. Thousands of moving parts must all come together to an exact departure minute. The pressure that everyone feels to make schedule is enormous, especially when unexpected snafus occur such as mechanical issues, weight and balance glitches, or extra bags to gate check.

Shortly after I heard that veteran lineman speak, I was sitting in the cockpit and getting ready to fly a five-day trip. Three minutes prior to scheduled departure, we still had approximately 10 minutes worth of work to do to finish the checklists for a maintenance issue. The pressure to perform was building in the cockpit as we began to instinctively push ourselves to hurry. To make matters worse, the airline company agent came into the cockpit with the final paperwork and in a slightly out-of-breath manner asked, "Can you give me an on-time departure?"

The pressure was immediately released when the captain looked at her and said, "We will do our professional best, but I am afraid we are going to be about 10 minutes late." Next he turned to me sitting in the copilot's seat and said, "Jeff, I want you to work at your normal pace. Do not rush anything. We cannot afford to miss a critical step because we are trying to save 10 minutes." After he said that, the company agent leaned forward and said, "Captain, I'll be waiting back in the jetway. Just let me know when you are ready to go." And with that, all the pressure to perform was completely deflated. We pushed back eight minutes late but did not miss a single item. The captain handled every single pressure cooker situation in the same measured, methodical pace. He was quick to recognize and then vocalize when he sensed pressure to perform beginning to build. His action in the cockpit was the epitome of a Target Leader setting the tone for how the work should be done when pressure mounts. Moreover, how company leadership reacts to decisions operators in the field make to slow down or stop work is directly related to creating a ZERO accident culture, or not.

To help pilots take their time when an emergency arises, they are taught to "wind the clock." Before state-of-the-art automation and navigation equipment, all cockpits had mechanical clocks that the pilot manually wound before each flight. Throughout our intense flight training, when faced with a situation, whether large or small, that caused us to mentally lose focus, our instructors instilled in us the need to wind the clock.

The phrase is now a metaphor. It means to slow down, take a breath, get your emotions under control, and assess the situation. You need to take the time to think logically and then work methodically to address the problem. Metaphorically speaking, to wind the clock means to fly the airplane first, no matter what. This helps pilots manage the impulsive/reactive side of the brain, especially when things seem completely out of control. Better decisions are made, both in and out of the cockpit, when the clock is wound.

So when things go haywire, how does an entire organization wind the clock before taking action? Let's consider the example of a utility power company. When a storm knocks out power, the local power company must spring into action to repair the damage. There's a lot of pressure on the company and its employees to restore power. The operator's instrument panel is buzzing and blinking with warnings and outage lights. Frightened and frustrated customers are calling.

Businesses are losing money when the power is out. Streetlights are not working, so public safety on the roads is a concern. And, of course, the power company itself is not generating revenue because the meters outside homes and businesses are not spinning.

In these instances, does the utility company leadership encourage the line crews to slow down and wind the clock before tackling each job? If the work crews restore power in record time, how does company leadership respond? Does the company ask probing questions such as "How did your team restore the power so quickly without violating safety procedures?" or does it pat the work crews on the back for doing the work so quickly? Leadership should not silently condone behavior they are normally not willing to tolerate. Company leadership must be vigilant to investigate that work was done properly and safely before rewarding employees for accomplishing work in record time. Failing to do so would send a mixed message.

Manufacturers are under pressure to produce goods faster when demand increases. When management considers pushing the production line to move faster, they would profit by first winding the clock. With that critical step back to assess the situation, the pressure is put on the employees to do their work and still be able to identify and resolve problems. The employees are not working at capacity—they're working above capacity—and the pressure to keep up is intense. If an employee drops something between moving belts or into a machine with moving parts, how will he or she react? Is the employee working so quickly that he or she will reactively reach into the moving equipment to retrieve the dropped item?

Winding the clock in these instances means having the ability to stop production without fear of reprisal or retribution in order to safely identify and address safety concerns. This can be effectively accomplished only through consistent training, steady reinforcement, and a production cycle that gives people enough time to think clearly under pressure.

Raising awareness about personal pressures to perform gets our attention. What gets our personal attention gets our focus and understanding.

A large construction company I was working with experienced the collapse of some heavy scaffolding because the crew felt pressured to get it assembled. Had someone taken the time to slow down, step back, and see the big picture, he or she would have clearly seen that it was being assembled incorrectly. Pressure to perform has led to many preventable accidents.

Remember to step back and use foresight 20/20/20: every 20 minutes, take 20 seconds and look 20 feet around.

Although it may seem counterintuitive, going slower is often quicker. When we slow down, we can actually save time (and possibly lives) by avoiding costly mistakes. As an opera-tor, when lights are flashing, buzzers are buzzing, and the hairs on the back of your neck are standing straight up, stepping back from the situation may be the one thing that will save you.

Companies don't push people; people push people.

When I hear people complain that their company is pushing them too hard to "get it done," potentially compromising safety, I think to myself, "Companies don't push people to get it done; people push people to get it done." Organizations don't fly airplanes, make decisions, drive forklifts, build intergalactic milkshake mixers, work on assembly lines, climb power poles, drill for oil, build houses, assemble widgets, or sit in board meetings; people do.

However, if the employee perceives that the company is pushing him or her to *get it done* at all costs, then that perception of reality is no differ-ent from that of the seven-year-old child who thinks there are monsters in the closet. It's up to Target Leaders to change those employees' perceptions, especially in areas of safety.

Is the message that Target Leaders send employees versus the message they receive the same? Leaders of companies must ensure that the message they send is exactly the message their employees receive. This type of reconciliation takes communication, inquiring, and understanding. Remember that beliefs and perceptions that affect lives are at stake. Figuratively speaking, it takes keeping one finger directly on the pulse of your employees and another finger directly on the pulse of the company to make sure everyone's heart is pulsing to the same beat.

The way it is done vs. the way it should be done.

I remember talking with a construction manager who was grappling with mixed messages he was unknowingly sending his crew. The crew was getting the message from him to *get it done faster,* which increased the pressure to perform and in turn led to an increase in injuries. The manger had to change the perceptions of his work crew.

He said he changed the way he phrased certain questions. For example, when he would ask his crew "When are you going to finish this project?" the phrasing of this question sent an unintended message to hurry up, work faster, get it done. This was not his intent. Instead, he now asks, "I have to schedule the next delivery of materials for this project; when do you suggest I have the materials delivered?" His intention all along was to keep new materials coming in ahead of time in order to keep the project moving. By understanding how his message was being received by his team, he was able to negate the workers' perception that he meant for them to hurry. By regularly checking the pulse of our people as well as the pulse of company values, we send a message that will be exactly the one received.

Companies are unfeeling legal entities that exist on paper and whose bottom line is to make money for shareholders. If a company had the power of speech and you were to ask it "How much money do you want to make next year?" it would answer with one word: "MORE." Greedy companies would answer with three words: "MORE, MORE, MORE." Those are the facts, not feelings.

However, people are what make up the "feelings" part of a company. Employees are the heart, the soul, and the lifeblood of the company. Interestingly, if you were to ask the people "How much do you want to make next year?" they would probably give the same answer as the company: "MORE."

On the surface, both the company and the people who work to sustain it seemingly want the same thing—MORE. We as Target Leaders, however, must stay ever mindful of one big difference. "More" to the company is based on bottom-line fact, which is profit and loss. That is black and white. What "more" means to the people who make up the company is not so clear-cut. "More" to you might mean something different from what it means to me.

Some employees want more time off from work; others may want more pay or better benefits. Some want more respect, more of a challenge, or more responsibility. Others may want a promotion, a job transfer, or newer equipment. This creates an interesting dilemma for Target Leaders when it comes to adding "more" to the bottom line of the company and giving "more" to the bottom line of the employees. On the one hand, companies need more money to grow, reinvest, gain market share, and update infrastructure to stay competitive. On the other hand, the people want more in order to increase their quality of life. Shareholders want higher returns; executives want bonuses; and employees want more time off, pay raises, and more benefits. I have seen incredibly wealthy companies profiting at the expense of employee morale, safety, and happiness. I have also seen companies struggling to survive while the employees refuse to budge on wage concessions, all because both sides want more. We must remind ourselves that everything is a balancing act.

I gave a presentation to a group of Target Leaders at a Fortune 500 company in Chicago. To underline the very difficult task they have of balancing the priorities between the company and its people, I hired a professional juggler to help make my point. I didn't hire just any juggler; I wanted a really good one. I wanted one with skill and experience and one who could perform under pressure. I asked him for references, which I verified before hiring him.

I wanted him to juggle five beanbags for a specified length of time. I asked him to juggle four blue beanbags and one green beanbag. The four blue bags represented:

- Quality
- Production/manufacturing
- Reliability/maintenance
- Environment/community

The fifth bag, the green bag, represented the safety and well-being of each employee. I gave the juggler a clear, measurable, and achievable directive. I said, "No matter what, don't drop the green bag. If you drop any of the blue bags, stop the work, reset yourself, analyze what went wrong, fix the problem, and then start juggling again."

And with that, the juggler set about doing what millions of Target Leaders do every day: expertly juggling many priorities without dropping any of them, especially the green one. Like a professional juggler, each of us must, on a daily basis, demonstrate absolute concentration, adroit skill, and expert training to juggle these different aspects of our work. It takes rhythm and timing. It means staying focused and keeping your eyes on all the beanbags. It means overcoming interruptions and distractions to keep everything moving in the right direction.

If the name of the tune is "The Safety Dance" but everyone is dancing "The Production Get-It-Done Jig," then the company Target Leaders need to change everyone's perception from the top down. I have seen many companies replace signs that showed their productivity numbers, once displayed as an indicator of winning, with signs indicating the number of days since the last injury. This is a way of realigning the tune with the dance. The safety numbers are used as a measure of performance instead of productivity. Companies have found that a quality product will come as a consequence of an efficient and safe work environment. Selling safety is sometimes difficult. It is difficult to assign a measurable figure to the number of injuries or accidents that were prevented as a result of installing a certain safety system or new initiative. Do you remember how many accidents you have prevented? All of them!

I was speaking to a company that was having difficulty at one of its work sites with employee slips, trips, and falls, especially when using stairs. What seemed to be a minor problem was beginning to cause real concern as the number of incidents was increasing. Everyone there was being a leader but not a Target Leader. The pressure to do more with less was affecting how the employees did their work. I was told that workers would carry big armloads of boxes, which obstructed their vision of the path in front of their feet, yet no one offered help. Handrail use was not encouraged. Poor shop housekeeping invited tripping hazards, and wet floors encouraged slipping.

To help eliminate slips, trips, and falls on the job, the company identified a few Target Leaders to help change people's perceptions about the simple routine act of walking and climbing stairs. They came up with the slogan "Walking Is Work." The purpose was to change employee perceptions about the simple act of walking.

The Target Leaders set a goal to eliminate all slipping and tripping hazards within six months. They worked to gain all the necessary knowledge to understand the issue and identify possible solutions. They even consulted with outside experts to identify things not previously noticed. They solicited input from within and used their own experiences to develop a plan. They set a vision of zero slips, trips, or falls by the end of six months. They empowered everyone to be a Target Leader and be involved in the program to implement the process that would achieve the shared goal.

Now, when an employee has an armload of boxes and is going up or down the stairs without using the handrail and other employees see this, they say something and go to help. This action not only reinforces the message that "walking is work" but also changes behaviors. The company went from having at least an incident per month to one per six months, a dramatic result. Their goal is zero.

What the company did was *picture its perfect.*

FIFTEEN

PICTURE YOUR
PERFECT

I talk to myself all the time. Sometimes it is a casual chat with a friend or coworker inside my head. Sometimes it's a heated debate between what is rational and irrational, what is ideal and what is real, or what is emotional and what is logical. Every so often, a funny thought will come to mind that I verbalize and then chuckle over. If I happen to be in a public place, people will stare at me as if I'm having a conversation with a leprechaun.

A debate I had with myself one time was trying to figure out why I have animated debates with myself. I concluded that I am usually trying to discern what is real and what is ideal. I will verbally debate how best to close the gap between what is achievable (reality) and what is desired (perfection). This is how I picture my perfect. Sometimes I will rehearse the perfect speech or have the perfect conversation. In the air force, we called this bit of odd behavior "chair flying." As a fighter pilot, I would sit in a chair and literally "chair fly" the perfect mission. I would think through each phase of the flight, to include verbalizing the radio calls to all the controlling agencies in the target area. I would rehearse which weapons to use to mitigate anticipated threats. I would talk myself through all the different layers of contingencies, asking "what if" questions and then answering them as if it were all happening in real time.

Whenever we make a plan, we have an outcome in mind. We have a picture in our mind's eye of what our perfect ending will be when we reach our goal. In that way, each of us creates our own personal picture of perfect every day. Picturing your perfect brings things into focus and helps you bring about the change you seek. It enables you to lay down the vision and expectations necessary for you to get where you want to go both personally and professionally.

When you desire to make a change for the better, you must consider many things when choosing the best route to get there. You might be trying to decide which new leadership program to introduce to your company. You might be struggling with implementing a new or different safety program for your employees. You might be deciding on a new exercise or diet program. When deciding which program works best, the short answer is the one you can commit to!

Picturing and pointing ourselves toward perfect also encourages us think about what the word "perfect" means. For me, perfection is the best possible version of the result I need. It's personal and requires a bit of inward reflection. Your pictured perfect could include:

- Achieving zero accidents at work or home.
- Increasing sales goals by 5% each quarter.
- Losing a set number of pounds per month until you're down to a healthy weight.
- Communicating more clearly with your spouse.
- Spending more time with your children
- Breaking a bad habit.
- Being more approachable at work.
- Following through with commitments.

Back in chapter 4, I gave many of you a reader's "stutter step" when I said that I believed all accidents are preventable. When picturing your perfect, it is best to set the bar high when pursuing perfection. Many companies are picturing their perfect as achieving a sustainable zero accident rate for all employees. In early 2003, one of my first major clients was the Southern Company, the parent corporation of a group of utility companies including Georgia Power, Alabama Power, Mississippi Power, and Gulf Power. Back then, senior leadership at each of these companies was struggling with how best to pursue perfection when it came to preventing incidents, accidents, and fatalities throughout all of the Southern Companies. Of course, the company's leadership knew what their perfect was: *zero accidents every minute of every day throughout the entire company.* Many thought zero accidents was an unattainable goal and setting such a goal was doomed to fail before beginning. The debate raged between "target zero accidents" and "target zero unsafe acts." The struggle was between what is perceived as possible (zero unsafe acts) and what is perceived as impossible (zero accidents). After much deliberation and consternation, senior leadership felt that "target zero unsafe acts" did not truly reflect their definition of pursuing perfection. They felt that "target zero accidents" was their picture-perfect vision for future business success. Thus, the new initiative "Target Zero" was born and participation by every employee was mandatory.

Trying to define "perfect" so that others will believe in it, embrace it, and strive for it as the new standard can be very difficult. How could Target Leaders throughout the Southern Companies make this goal achievable? The first step was communication. Through a series of road shows they communicated the fact that if the entire company went even two minutes without an accident, then the goal of zero had been achieved. Seen in that light, perfect was now believable and achievable. If the entire company could reach two minutes, then it was possible to expand the accident-free period to four minutes. Keep raising the bar!

"If we can go four minutes without an accident, then we can go eight," they continued. They could then translate this into hours, weeks, months, and years. They integrated that fighter pilot attitude, continuously raising the bar to beat the previous milestone. It was critical to their success to ensure that the leadership at all levels truly embraced the concept of Target Zero, owned it, and, most importantly, believed in it personally. All that they achieved came through unified investment and shared focus. Remember that what gets our attention gets our focus and then gets done.

I was fortunate to have been at the inception of the Target Zero initiative at the Southern Companies. I was honored when they chose me to help spread the marching tune of "Target Zero" throughout their organization.

People might forget the words to a song, but they remember the tune. What is the tune you want others to hum throughout the day?

All levels had to embrace the concept. It was the only way to truly carry the message from the highest to the lowest levels, the levels where lives were on the line. The Target Zero initiative was an expectation of perfection that brought responsibility and accountability to every individual throughout the company.

Finally, each of the Southern Companies measured its success. Just as we did in our fighter pilot debriefs, they measured trends, habits, and deviations from best practices. They also measured the hours, days, weeks, and months between less than zero moments, noting any patterns. What was the beginning of the trend? Could they spot and enhance or correct indicators and trends? If they landed short of the target, they simply reset the Target Zero clock and started the count again. Since 2003, their lost-time injuries and accident rates have fallen so dramatically that future improvements have become more difficult to achieve each year, yet they still strive for perfection, Target Zero. In February 2012, the Nuclear Regulatory Commission (NRC) approved the Southern Company's plan to build two nuclear reactors at Plant Vogtle, south of Augusta, Georgia. This approval was a monumental achievement. It was the first time approval by the NRC to build nuclear reactors had been granted in almost 35 years (since 1978). This historic approval came as a testament to the faith the NRC was putting in the Southern Company's people to build and operate a safe, reliable, and efficient nuclear plant.

———

Be the change you seek in the world.

—**Gandhi**

———

When companies picture their perfect by defining an aggressive initiative such as Target Zero, it will simply fall on deaf ears unless they develop a plan to drive the change they seek. As Target Leaders, our job is to inspire the belief in ourselves and others that the new vision is possible.

If you always do what you've always done, you will always get what you've always gotten.

Changing results means changing behaviors. To drive positive change means understanding the indicators and behaviors that accentuate progress toward our perfect. Just as importantly, we must also understand how to reduce or eliminate the drivers that impede our vision of perfect. We know that our actions often foreshadow the future. If we behave in a certain way, the outcome will reflect these behaviors. These behaviors and the predictive outcomes are called indicators; they point to, or *indicate*, the outcome, and that outcome can be positive or negative. Target Leaders strive to identify both positive and negative indicators and then work to replicate the positive and eliminate the negative.

———

To work in the service of life and living, in search of the answers to questions unknown. To be part of the movement and part of the growing, is part of beginning to understand.

—John Denver, 1975 Tribute to Jacques-Yves Cousteau and his research ship, the *Calypso*

———

In the business of life, Target Leaders encourage us to pay attention to the leading indicators that may ultimately predict where a potential accident or problem might occur. The idea is to be as proactive as you can and push the fight in trying to prevent future mishaps. This is analogous to looking out the windshield of your car. It means looking ahead to determine when to speed up or slow down or watch out for bumps and curves.

Creating a leading indicator program (LIP) empowers employees of an organization to speak up about all the little things that can potentially lead up to a big thing. I say, "Give it LIP." An example of the LIP process is when the

Federal Aviation Administration (FAA) began identifying potential problem areas called "hot spots." These are specific areas at each airport where the FAA believed a runway incursion was most likely to happen. An incursion occurs when a taxiing aircraft moves onto an active runway without proper clearance and potentially collides with another aircraft taking off or landing. Once the FAA identified those leading indicators, it pinpointed the hot spots with bright red circles on all airport taxi charts so pilots are readily able to identify areas where a potential incursion might occur.

———

In October 2010, the Federal Aviation Administration announced the number of runway incursions in the United States had dropped by half since the previous year.

—**Chapin, R. 2010.** *Runway incursions 2000–2010: Is safety improving?* **Retrieved from** http://www.miqrogroove.com/writing/runway-incursions/

———

Conversely, lagging indicators are based on events that have already occurred. These are the incidents and accidents that are now behind us, as in looking out of our rearview mirror. Being aware of past occurrences does help us predict future problems; however, lagging indicators are reactive in nature because the lessons are learned only after a mishap has occurred.

Creating a LIP program proactively "pushes the fight" to head off potential incidents and accidents before they occur, not after. ExxonMobil's "Nobody Gets Hurt" campaign enables the company to monitor behaviors and analyze processes to ensure the highest level of safety. Employees are empowered at any time to voice their concerns about unsafe activities and practices or other areas of work. It is an expectation within that behemoth company to track all the leading indicators to pursue "nobody gets hurt" perfection.

It is better to watch the gas gauge to make sure we do not run out of fuel than it is to run out of fuel and then watch the gauge!

Unfortunately, many companies pay "lip service" to safety without the follow-through necessary to create a solid culture that protects people, property, and product. And there may be an old-school attitude of "if it's not broken, don't fix it." A LIP will address the issue of safety follow-up through the most knowledgeable source available to them—the employee, the man or woman who is actually on the job doing the hands-on work. That worker understands what is actually done and not done, what works and does not work, and what is safe and not safe in the workplace. The worker's knowledge can provide the means to an effective deterrent to accidents and injuries.

A good LIP will create and implement measures and incentives that encourage employees to speak up when they see a problem. The Target Leaders must establish a culture of mutual respect and trust so that employees know their concern will be considered and, certainly, no disciplinary action will come down for reporting it. Armed with this inside, vital information, the LIP can effectively eliminate hazards in the workplace. BAM!

How do you establish a LIP? The first step is to create a team that will oversee the LIP. This group should represent a cross-organizational team committed to improving safety performance throughout the company. Team membership may include:

- Union/employee members
- Corporate/management members
- Support staff members
- Line workers/drivers or others involved in day-to-day operations

The purpose of the LIP team is to identify and reduce deviations from approved work practices, detect unsafe acts, and implement corrective measures to better manage the risks associated with the job. In doing so, the LIP will enhance safety through the prevention of accidents and incidents and encourage the voluntary reporting of safety issues and events that occur on the job. For example, an oil rig managed by a major oil company had a message board where employees could write job issues for the LIP team to review and develop possible actions and solutions. The LIP may recommend a change in procedures, staffing, or reviews to ensure greater safety levels. Finally, the LIP team can—and should—be empowered to establish a team to implement such decisions and recommendations.

Submissions to the LIP team by employees should have a formal guarantee of immunity from punishment. The reports of unsafe or questionable events are submitted to the LIP committee within a certain time frame, say, in 48 hours of the event or observation. As well, the reporting employee should have immunity unless he or she was involved in:

- Criminal activity
- Drug, alcohol, or controlled substance use
- Intentional falsification
- Wanton or reckless disregard for safety

Establish a process: A typical LIP process might begin with the employee submitting a report through a web interface. Once that is completed, the employee will receive written confirmation—via e-mail, letter, or other means—of the submission. The report will be received anonymously by the LIP committee, which sometimes requires a third party to remove identifying details. The LIP committee will then review the report and background information, discuss, and make recommendations. A process is established to give the employee and company feedback and suggestions to remedy the situation. Such resolutions or actions may include:

- More individual or employee group training
- Better personal protection equipment (PPE)
- Improved vehicle awareness
- Rule changes or enhancement
- Equipment upgrades or replacement
- Reinforcement of current policies
- Employee debriefing and/or mentoring with regard to the occurrence

The solutions recommended by the LIP can vary depending on the situation, the track record of the employee, and other factors. However, the committee should have clear criteria by which to decide a course of action. The challenge may be that this information is in different manuals, files, and other locations throughout the business. You may have to be a combination of librarian and detective to figure out where all of the information about various procedures is housed. If someone gets hurt, the team goes back and researches all the manuals. Another book may contain a policy guidance that the operating crew did not know about, or maybe the crew didn't expand its research to find that piece of information.

—⟨∾∾⟩—

It may seem counter-intuitive, but federal aviation officials said Wednesday they will make the skies safer for air travelers by not punishing FAA employees who report making mistakes, but by protecting them from punishment. FAA officials announced that as part of a new "safety culture" at the agency, they would fully embrace non-punitive reporting systems, in an effort to generate information that could expose bigger dangers. The FAA created a non-punitive reporting system for air traffic controllers in 2008, and now extends that program to employees who maintain radar installations and other systems. "Operational errors" will now be known as "operational incidents". The change will reduce the stigma associated with errors, thereby increasing information and allowing the agency to make life-saving changes.

—http://www.cnn.com/2012/03/14/travel/faa-nonpunitive-reporting/index.html?htp-hp_bn9

—⟨∾∾⟩—

It's important to note that many times, the leading and lagging indicators show us only the tip of the iceberg. But they're the primary way we can avoid the sizable risk that can be represented as the main mass of the iceberg submerged below the water's surface.

The most vital part of making use of leading indicators is ensuring accountability for addressing the issues. It does no good to picture our perfect if we fail to put mechanisms in place to measure our performance. Ideally, the consequences in this area will be positive (a positive review comment, an organizational acknowledgement, or a bonus of some sort for success) rather than negative (penalties for failure to improve). When the focus is on the positive, the use of leading indicators to improve overall performance has a stronger possibility of becoming systemic and part of the culture.

How should employees handle a situation where one of their own attempts to stray off the desired perfect path? Target Leader speaker and marine F-18 pilot Wes Sharp often refers to the phrase "Keep off the marine corps' grass" as an illustration of how a large organization, made up of many people at many different levels, creates a culture that encourages speaking up when others deviate from the desired path.

When Wes first joined the marines, he was told that no one was permitted to "cut across the marine corps' grass." He thought it was simply another rule to make his life more difficult. "Besides," he said, "the grass at many marine corps bases looked terrible. If the marines cared so much about their lawn, then why didn't they take better care of it?" Not only that but some marine bases didn't have grass at all, yet they would comb smooth an area of sand or gravel and then line the area with rocks and post a sign that said, "Keep off the grass."

As a young marine officer, Wes was running late for a meeting one day. He decided to take a shortcut and deviate from the designated path. He *cut across the grass*. Out of nowhere he heard a voice that sounded like drill sergeant R. Lee Ermey of *Full Metal Jacket* fame: "Geeeet oooooff the mahhhhrine corps' graaaaass!"

Wes spun around, and there stood a young lance corporal, clearly junior in rank to him. The corporal witnessed someone deviate from the right path to the wrong path, and the culture empowered him to speak up. Right is right, and wrong is wrong. Wes, although a bit red-faced, had the courage to listen and stepped back onto the correct path, thus reinforcing the culture of pursuing the perfect path.

On the surface, this might seem petty, but on the field of battle, where it really counts, not only must everyone know and follow the rules but also all must have the courage to speak up to stay the correct path, no matter the rank. Footprints that cut across our organization's lawn are analogous to leading indicators. If the steps are allowed to continue, a worn footpath will soon develop.

Military aviators use the phrase "Knock it off" to immediately stop the work. When we hear it, it's as if somebody has snapped a finger and you instantly stop what you're doing. You don't ask why. You don't roll your eyes. You don't say, "Well, hang on a minute." It's a means of calling a time-out to make sure everyone is on the same path.

When a fighter pilot hears "Knock it off" over the radio, "it is like a verbal SLAP to the brain":

- **S**top the work immediately.
- **L**isten to concerns with an open mind.
- **A**ssess the situation and evaluate the validity of the concern.
- **P**roceed after all concerns are answered and situational awareness is congruent with reality.

A few years ago, I introduced the phrase "Knock it off" and the SLAP concept to utility giant Pacific Gas and Electric (PG&E). During a series of conferences and workshops, I spoke to more than 5,000 International Brotherhood of Electrical Workers (IBEW) Local 1245 electrical union members throughout California. Tom Dalzell, the president of the union, and several members of the union leadership team joined forces with me to work on picturing their perfect in the context of their business. I conducted several workshops called "Knock It Off."

From that vision, Tom put his union safety committee into action by holding a series of peer-to-peer focus groups to figure out how best to create and implement an initiative that would help reduce injuries and accidents among the IBEW brotherhood. Electrical workers face a high risk of injury on the job. Employees routinely string or replace great lengths of heavy electrical cable, and the risk of physical injury or death from electrocution is ever present. This is serious business; workplace accidents had taken the lives of 10 Local 1245 linemen in the previous seven years (http://www.ibew1245.com/news-Safety/Hold_the_Pull_9-30-10.html).

With input, discussion, and suggestions from everyone involved, the IBEW Local 1245 eventually pictured its perfect by creating a peer-to-peer mentoring program called Hold the Pull. As one committee member said, "Hold the Pull is a program created by linemen for linemen." When utility lineman are pulling miles of wire using powerful wenches and someone says "Hold the pull," they know it means to immediately stop the powerful drum wench. Like "Knock it off," it is a verbal brain SLAP to instantly stop! Every crew member is empowered to speak up, no matter his or her level of experience.

The Hold the Pull campaign was implemented in the face of a number of challenges, including:

- Aging power line infrastructure.
- Many new linemen.
- Young employees who seemed to come from an easily distracted generation.
- An industry trying to increase productivity while reducing the workforce.
- A workforce composed of highly confident and self-assured individuals.

Planning and implementing a campaign for a company as big as PG&E were neither simple nor quick. A program that large required a stepped approach to define the goal, put the necessary processes and safeguards in place, measure the performance, and be accountable for the results. Once the protocol had been defined, the union Target Leaders communicated the new program throughout the entire organization through a series of DVDs, workshops, road shows, posters, briefings, and other forms of internal communication.

The program has now grown beyond just linemen. I recently spoke to Ralph Armstrong, assistant business manger of IBEW Local 1245, and he said, "Hold the Pull is so successful that we have now started Control the Pressure for gas workers and another peer-to-peer program for line clearance tree trimmers called Keep the Clearance." All are currently in different stages of development and implementation. The picture-perfect vision of reducing injuries among union workers has the attention of other utility companies looking to implement similar programs within their union ranks.

So, when you are ready to picture your perfect, don't be afraid to have a lively debate with yourself. Go ahead! Pace back and forth, and stab your finger into the air with each point you make. Shake your head, roll your eyes, kick the dirt, shrug your shoulders, put your hands on your hips, raise an eyebrow, laugh a little, smirk a bit, and pooch your lips, too. Just don't do it in a public institution, unless you already are in a public institution.

SIXTEEN

SPEED RUSH
BASELINE

I f you drove down a completely unrestricted, open, and endless road at 70 mph, would you appreciate how fast you were really going? Probably not because you drive 70 mph almost every day. At 70 mph, you cover the length of two football fields in six seconds. Are you impressed now? I doubt it because driving 70 mph, no matter how you slice it, is just not that impressive. That's why we see people driving while eating a burger, shaving, putting on makeup, texting, or having animated conversations with themselves.

What if you were traveling down the same unrestricted road at 400 mph—would you appreciate how fast you were going then? Absolutely! What if you drove the same unrestricted road at that speed for eight to 10 hours a day, five days a week, for 10 years—would you appreciate how fast you were going then? Probably not.

Fighter pilots refer to this phenomenon as "speed rush baseline." We get so used to flying at very high speeds day in and day out that going fast

165

is normal to us. We simply fail to appreciate how fast we are traveling. This is a normal occurrence experienced by everyone. It is caused by "optical flow," a mechanism within our brains that senses motion. Anytime we are traveling at one speed over long periods of time, our brains adjust to the speed, which establishes our "baseline." If we increase the speed, our brains quickly adjust and establish the higher speed as the new baseline. However, the opposite is true if we slow down. We do not want to adjust to a slower speed because our brain senses a disproportionate change in the optical flow. It is a strong, tempting desire to speed up again and reestablish an ever-higher speed baseline.

Let's apply speed rush baseline to our personal and professional lives. Think back to when you were first hired. Like driving a car for the first time, everything was new and the days seemed to go by in a hurry. You wanted to learn quickly, and you did your job well. You were eager to soak up information, watch others, listen, and learn. Your goal was to figure out how things were supposed to be done so that you didn't make mistakes and get fired or injured. Each day that passed, you accelerated your job performance a little bit more, establishing a new baseline.

Career advancement is a slow process that progresses over time, month by month. After two years of slowly accelerating in your career to, say, 70 mph, it no longer seems very fast to you because the speed increases so gradually over a long period of time. Because our brain does not want to slow down or do anything that would put the brakes on our career, we fail to appreciate how fast we are really traveling not only within ourselves but also in relation to those around us.

Pretend you are standing on the side of the road and a car driving by at 70 mph misses you by one inch. You would certainly appreciate how fast 70 mph was then! Put this into career perspective and think of all the new people in your organization standing on the side of the road and watching you whiz by them within inches at 70 mph. Appreciating who you are to them means appreciating the speed you are traveling in relation to those around you. Some might be traveling the same speed as you, some at 400 mph, and others at 5 mph. Target Leaders inspire their people to realize the importance of keeping their speeds in perspective relative to themselves and their surroundings.

When I was flying the T-6 with my brother on the air show circuit, I failed to appreciate the speed I was traveling relative to his speed. In my mind, I was just plodding along. But he, as a nonpilot, saw me whiz by at 70 mph, and when we flew, he took his cues from me. On the other hand, Johnny was a licensed building contractor, and each winter when we weren't flying air shows together, I would help him remodel homes. All of a sudden, he was the one flying at 70 mph, and I was the one standing still on his job site. He was the foreman, he knew what to do and how to do it, and he could do it fast. When he needed a gopher, I was his man. I could go-fer nails, or go-fer tools, or go-fer water because that was just my speed. If he took a shortcut or used the wrong tool for a job, I trusted his judgment. If he told me to hold the ladder while he teetered near the top rung, I did it without question. If he used the table saw without ear or eye protection, I figured he knew what he was doing.

As a supervisor at work, you might think you're just poking along in your career car, but those around you see and feel the speed at which you are traveling. Marine F-18 fighter pilot and fellow Target Leadership speaker Wes Sharp uses this analogy to great effect when he speaks to company employees. During his presentation, he shows the audience a current picture of himself as a balding senior-ranking officer sitting in the cockpit of his F-18 fighter. He points to the picture and says, "When I first joined the marines, I had a full head of hair; now look at me!" The audience chuckles as Wes continues, "In this picture, I'm officially one of the old guys." He then brings the group back to a time and place when he was a brand-new lieutenant. Back then, he clearly remembers thinking to himself, "Man, I'll never be that old! Those pilots are so old they have one foot in the grave and the other on a banana peel!"

He also remembers looking up to those old guys. In his mind they were traveling at blistering speeds. He studied all their flying techniques; he watched how they carried themselves; he paid attention to their character and listened to their advice. Some were better leaders and better officers than others. He held onto the good qualities and let go of the bad. Today he looks at himself as one of the old guys, in a humble sort of way. At this point, he truly appreciates who he is and the speed he's traveling compared to those junior to him.

I once heard a funny story involving Muhammad Ali, one of the greatest boxers of all time. At the height of his career, he had boarded an airplane and was sitting in his first-class seat. Just before takeoff, one of the flight attendants noticed he wasn't wearing his seat belt. She politely asked him to "buckle up for takeoff," to which he responded with light-hearted confidence, "I'm Superman, and Superman doesn't need a seat belt." To which the flight attendant replied, "Superman doesn't need an airplane, either, so you need to buckle up."

Ali's optimism and confidence are legendary, but in this instance even he had to be reminded to check his personal speedometer to stay firmly anchored in reality. With this in mind, when you find areas where you're weak, focus on the skills you need and surround yourself with people who have these strengths. Many people find it easy to identify their strengths but have a very difficult time being honest with themselves about their areas of weakness. Once you have made an accurate self-assessment, you can go to your mentors and say, "This is an area where I'd like to increase my skills. I've noticed that you're very good at this. Would you be willing to work with me in this area?"

I've done that myself a number of times with people I trust and respect. They may not have known how much I looked up to them until I told them how fast they were traveling relative to me. Honest praise helps the people around you know what they are doing right. Checking your personal speedometer means understanding your strengths and weaknesses, which can then help you see the curves and speed bumps you might face when driving toward your lifetime goals.

Experience helps us choose the right path, and confidence helps us move forward on that path.

With increased speed comes increased responsibility. Think of the many sports heroes who have failed to appreciate the incredible speed they were traveling and did not change their behavior to accommodate that speed. For example, Michael Vick failed to appreciate the importance of the speed of his character when he ran afoul of the law while playing for the Atlanta Falcons.

His arrest on felony dogfighting charges and subsequent time spent in prison ground his career to a dead stop. Lawyers' fees and punitive fines ruined him financially. After Vick's release from prison, he was mentored by former Indianapolis Colts coach Tony Dungy, whose coaching strategy puts faith and family ahead of football and material things. Vick's career began to accelerate again, and in December 2009, he received the Ed Block Courage Award, as voted by his teammates. The award honors players who "exemplify commitment to the principles of sportsmanship and courage." It meant a great deal to Vick to receive the award by a unanimous vote. Another high flying example is Lance Armstrong. His cycling career is imploding around him simply because he failed to appreciate the speed he was traveling relative to those around him. He thought he was invincible. His crash is still unfolding around him, and will be for years to come.

Other examples are the speed at which greed overran many of our best and brightest corporate leaders. Many financial institutions suffered immeasurable damage, including Lehman Brothers, Merrill Lynch, and KPMG, after they implemented rules that enabled people to borrow far more than they could ever pay back in order to purchase a house. The end result was the collapse of the entire real estate market. The higher your position, the faster you're moving and the more attentive you need to be to what you do and how you do it. All types of leaders, from the boardroom, the military, and the government, would do well to take stock of their current actions and plans in order to avoid an "unintended hard impact," also known in the industry as a crash landing.

The higher we rise in life, the more important it is to stay grounded in reality and human nature. The faster we fly, the more careful we need to be in order to stay on course. It is vitally important to continually appreciate who we are in an objective and confident way but without arrogance. The more awareness we have of our own value and the value of those around us, the more in tune we will be with our leadership potential and our abilities to have a positive impact in all areas of life. Without a sense of speed, purpose, and impact, it's difficult to grasp and master the more complicated aspects of being a Target Leader.

I started flying planes when I was 14 and earned my commercial pilot's license at 18. By the time I graduated from college and joined the air force to become a pilot, I had 2,000 hours of flight time under my belt. I've now been flying planes for more than three decades. All that experience, knowledge, and training can bring about an egotistical attitude in the cockpit. Bravado and overconfidence can kill just as fast as being too comfortable and relaxed with the job. My attitude when I am flying commercially with an entire crew, flight attendants, and passengers on board must be as conscientious as when I'm by myself.

When my oldest son was 14 years old, he expressed an interest in learning to fly. I had to dial into my speed relative to his speed. When it came to flying an airplane, in my son's eyes he thought I could fly anything with both hands tied behind my back while doing barrel rolls through open hangar doors. At 14, he was at his most impressionable age—young and eager to learn and please his dad. I knew that my attitude and work behavior would serve as direct examples and reflections of my expectations of him. I emphasized to him that even though I hold an Airline Transport Pilot (ATP) license, the highest aviation rating given by the Federal Aviation Administration, it is nothing more than a license to learn. I also felt it was important to hire a certified flight instructor to give my son a different perspective.

Whether your goal is to be a crew chief, the CEO, or somewhere in between, Target Leadership principles will help you get there. We've already talked about how you can improve yourself and those around you by walking your talk, setting goals, and finding ways to inspire others through your leadership principles. In addition, Target Leaders benefit by surrounding themselves with positive people who support them in their goals and endeavors. It can sometimes seem like a dog-eat-dog world, which can cause you to react negatively and retreat from your principles. You may remember the movie *Jerry Maguire*, starring Tom Cruise. In that movie, Cruise's character, Jerry, pleads passionately, "Help me help you." That's just basic human psychology. For the most part, people are always seeking ways to improve, and when they have somebody who comes along to help them, then they in turn want to return the favor. But when you get involved in a situation where you really want to help others progress and achieve those small goals that are going to get you closer to your big goal, it can move you forward like a turbocharged jet engine.

The Target Leader at work knows that *desire* is probably the most powerful force in the world when it comes to getting things done—and done right. Desire has driven people to accomplish extraordinary feats. In our intense survival school during my air force training, we were shown how prisoners of war were able to endure horrific conditions and unimaginable torture not because they feared death but because they desired to live.

When we desire to do right by others, we will not speed, run red lights, rob banks, or cheat, simply because we want to do the right thing, not because we fear being caught. If we fear getting caught, we will do just enough to stay out of trouble and just the minimum needed to do what is right and good.

The desire to win is greater than our fear of losing.

Desire motivated and propelled our nation to the moon. On September 12, 1962, President Kennedy visited Rice University in Houston, Texas, where he gave his historic speech. President Kennedy tapped directly into our nation's desire to win the space race against the Russians by referring to a sport event, Rice's football rivalry with Texas.

"But why, some say, the moon? Why choose this as our goal? And they may well ask why climb the highest mountain? Why, 35 years ago, fly the Atlantic? Why does Rice play Texas?" President Kennedy tapped our desire to win by promising to put an American on the moon "before the decade is out." Our desire to reach this goal was greater than our fear of losing to the Russians, who, at that time, had a more advanced space program than we did. He inspired the desire in America to rise to the challenge, to reach for the stars, and to win.

———

We choose to go to the moon. We choose to go to the moon in this decade and do the other things not because they are easy but because they are hard, because that goal will serve to organize and measure the best of our energies and skills, because that challenge is one that we are willing to accept, one we are unwilling to postpone, and one which we intend to win.

—John F. Kennedy

———

Target Leaders who inspire desire find that their employees will do the work not because they fear losing their job or losing a bonus but because they want to do the work both for themselves and for the organization. Inspiring others this way isn't easy, but it is an indispensable trait every Target Leader must endeavor to acquire, hone, and retain. Remember to give a few minutes of public praise when someone succeeds. It is just as important to give your personal support when someone fails.

Understanding and appreciating your speed rush baseline relative to those around you will help you to become a better Target Leader.

SEVENTEEN

A NEW BROTHER

Less than a month after my brother Johnny was killed, a 23-year-old law student named Sean Bullard walked into my dad's office and sat down. Sean brought his girlfriend, Jennifer, also a law student, with him for support. There was tenseness in the air as Sean, a former Ole Miss football player, waited to meet my dad for the first time. Just as I had gazed at the walls of Colonel Cushenberry's office, Sean's and Jennifer's eyes scanned my dad's "I love me" wall, adorned with pictures, certificates, and plaques.

Jennifer pointed to a picture of Dad in a football uniform and whispered, "Look, Sean; it looks like Mr. Espenship played football at Florida State University."

"Yeah," Sean responded. He pointed to another picture and quietly said, "Look at that picture, Jennifer. It looks like he played professional football for the Montreal Allouettes, too."

Their conversation stopped when Dad walked in. Sean steadied his nerves and then began: "Mr. Espenship, my mom tells me that you are my father."

Sitting there in front of my dad was a living, breathing result of a temptation he had faced and a choice he had made with Sean's mother 23 years before. At the time of Sean's conception, my dad was a handsome, athletic, charismatic, and very successful general contractor in a small town. He and my mom were divorced at the time and he was flying down to Miami frequently to visit us and talk my mom into coming back to him. Unfortunately, when presented with temptations, he tended to make poor decisions. My dad handled Sean's startling accusation in the same manner he did when my mom accused him of having affairs when they were married. He admitted nothing, denied everything, made counteraccusations, and usually demanded an apology for being falsely accused.

In this case Dad could not deny or make counteraccusations against the DNA testing to which he reluctantly agreed. The results proved that Sean was indeed my dad's son. I had a new brother. Within a week of learning the results, Dad's friends sent him cigars and Hallmark cards with pictures of babies and storks. I was anxious to meet my new baby brother. When Sean and I met for the first time, we gave each other a long embrace. We had an instant blood bond. We spent a lot of time catching up and getting to know each other.

Growing up, Johnny was the only brother I knew until Sean summoned the courage to confront his paternal father. Sean's life without a dad was much more difficult than mine. I learned that he had two younger half brothers. Sadly, both died before I had a chance to meet them. One died of cancer, and the other died of a drug overdose. Those were the only brothers Sean had. Losing them left as big a void in Sean's life as losing Johnny left in mine. I was asking Sean the details about his brothers when we had an Oprah Winfrey "aha moment." Sean's youngest brother and I share the same birthday (although not the same birth year). Cue Rod Serling and roll the music from *The Twilight Zone*. We just sat and stared at each other. Could it be divine intervention, coincidence, and fate all rolled into one that his younger brother and I share the same birth date? Who knows. What Sean and I do know is that we are blessed to have each other.

Some of you are probably wondering what my mom thought of all this. Mom had divorced Dad some 20 years prior to this discovery, and she was not surprised at all when I told her. She burst into tears of joy for all of us because Sean was a part of me and a part of Johnny. Sean was my new brother, and Mom welcomed him into her life as if he were her own son.

Once, I wryly suggested to Sean that, considering the fact that I had lost my brother and he had lost both of his brothers, the odds of survival for being a brother to either of us were not good. He chuckled and wished me good luck at surviving. That was almost 20 years ago. Sean is still around, and so am I. Our bond is very close.

Sean wrote a book called *Casino's Gamble*. It is a fictional novel based on his personal life growing up in Jacksonville, Florida. Being raised without a father was a struggle for him, and I admire how he has achieved so much with so little. He put himself through college at Ole Miss on a football scholarship and worked his way through law school. He married his girlfriend, Jennifer, and together they run a successful private practice. Sean got by on grit, determination, and, most of all, courage. These are the same attributes my mom had when she left Dad with two little boys in tow.

Courage is making the right choice when the wrong choice appears easiest. Courage is stepping away from what is comfortable. Courage is leaving behind those things you once valued with faith that they will be gained again and will be even better then. Courage is taking one more step. Courage is standing back up when failure knocks you down. Courage is what gets you through one more day.

Through her courage, grit, and determination, Mom managed to raise two small boys to become grown young men. She serves as my Target Leader, role model, and mentor. She is as solid as they come and spot-on with her wisdom and advice.

As for my dad, he did the best he could with the character tools he had. Although marriage was not for him, he did care about his two boys. One thing he always did was to hug and kiss us hello and good-bye. When Johnny died, Dad was adamant that he would go to the morgue to hug and kiss his son good-bye. I went with him for support. The man in charge said Johnny was badly burned and his body was in no condition for viewing.

Dad was insistent and used his physical size and charged emotion to convince the man to open the door to the room where Johnny's body was being kept. Dad went in. I waited outside. Ten minutes later Dad came back out. I could see the trail his tears made through the ashes on his cheeks. I could see the ashes on his lips where he kissed his eldest boy good-bye. I saw the ashes on his hands, his big arms, and his barreled chest where he scooped his son up and held his body tightly for the last time. The 10 minutes Dad spent with Johnny intensely affected his life in a negative way. Dad's physical and mental health degraded day by day. Gradually, he emotionally walled everyone out of his life, except for me. At times he even tries to block me out and he continues to refuse all offers of help. Losing Johnny in an airplane crash and kissing him good-bye *profoundly* affected Dad's life, and it all began with failing to pull a propeller blade through to check for hydraulic lock.

As painful as it is for me to write about this, my hope is that sharing the story of my brother's loss will underscore that you are also in the business of profoundly affecting others. You are a leader. As such, you influence the thoughts, actions, and decisions of those around you. As a Target Leader, you can also inspire and encourage others to make the right choice when a wrong choice seems easier or quicker. We all have a propeller blade to pull through, and I hope to inspire you to pull yours through every hour of every day.

EIGHTEEN

THE FINAL WORD

*I would like to give my mom the final word in this
last chapter. This is from her, in her own words.*

To our esteemed readers: if you have read this far, or if you are one who reads the end first, may I introduce myself. I am Mom. I want to tell you right up front that I represent millions of parents all over this world who have done all they knew how to give their children every advantage in life. This man you know as Odie, the pilot, speaker, and writer, who has asked his mom to write some words of wisdom in this last chapter of his book, is my son, Jeff. He and his brother Johnny are my success stories.

Odie wanted me to tell you about myself and my struggles raising two boys as a single mother and how I coped with the grief of losing our Johnny. Again, I represent millions of parents who have experienced life's struggles and who have lost children. I believe you might rather like to hear about Odie, who he is, and how he came to be standing before audiences speaking about leadership and safety. So, I will briefly weave both of those themes, a bit about our lives and struggles, together with Odie's personality into this short chapter. You may see yourself or someone you know in our life story because, as Ecclesiastes 1:9 NIV wisely states, "What has been will be again, what has been done will be done again; there is nothing new under the sun."

Jeffrey came as a surprise, born almost 15 months after his brother, Johnny. So close in age, the two boys soon became inseparable. Jeffrey was both entertained by and at the mercy of his older brother. He quickly learned how to take orders and play fair. The same could not be said for their father and me. Realizing that I might have to support my boys some day, I borrowed money from my parents and completed college with a degree in elementary education. Soon, my husband's alcohol use and its associated vices led to divorce, and I and the boys moved to Miami, Florida, near my family.

After securing a job as a second-grade teacher and enrolling Jeffrey and Johnny in first and second grades in a nearby school, I rented an apartment with a pool, close to our schools. That year, Dade County was complying with the desegregation of its schools by moving the newly hired teachers into the schools with all-black populations, rather than moving the children. I, therefore, was moved from my school near the boys to a distant school to teach third-grade children of migrant workers. It turned out to be the most difficult and most rewarding experience of my teaching career. I could easily devote a chapter to it. As hard as that year was, with the grief, turmoil, and upheaval, we kept our eyes on the bright side. I grew immensely as a teacher and learned to love and meet the needs of a very different student population than any I had experienced before. We were near my supportive family, we could go swimming all year, and the boys made friends with children in the apartments. When I mention the difficulties of those days, Jeff reminds me that he and Johnny had a great time. That tells me how resilient children can be. And I should mention here that it was during this time, when the boys' father was visiting us and courting me again, that a baby was conceived, but not with me. Had I known, what happened next would not have happened.

At the urging of their father and in an effort to keep our family together, the boys and I moved back to north Florida. Meanwhile, a baby boy was born to a single mother. His name is Sean. Although Sean shared the same father with Johnny and Jeffrey, we knew nothing of his existence until many years later.

Our second marriage lasted a few years but soon became evident that nothing had changed. I should point out here that even though life was not good for their dad and me, we kept our arguments fairly quiet. I believe it is OK for children to experience adults working out disagreements in a constructive way. But they do not need to be involved in the turmoil of adult arguments or hear unkind words exchanged between the two people they love most. Their dad and I divorced again.

The boys and I remained in the little north Florida town, where I bought a house across the street from the elementary school where I worked. The boys played baseball, usually on the same team, and had great support from the coaches who helped transport them to practice and games when I had to work. They had friends who lived on our street, and Jeff may have begun to learn some of his negotiating skills then. Our house was where the kids brought their disagreements. We'd sit down, talk about it, and try to figure out how to solve the problem. They were remarkably capable of working out solutions.

When the boys were in their early teens, I decided that I wanted them to know more of our beautiful country than the little town where we lived. I hocked a couple rings that I no longer wore and a mink stole that I definitely didn't need, and with the money, I bought a bright-orange used VW Westfalia Camper. We outfitted it with our camping gear, took a couple trips into the Georgia/North Carolina mountains, and hiked portions of the Appalachian Trail.

We traveled with a close neighbor, who was a teacher and single mother with two children and a gold VW camper. We bought CB radios to stay in touch with each other on the road, and the *Florida Orange* and the *Gold Medal* (we were headed for the Olympics) put the pedal to the metal and headed up the East Coast. We toured every historic landmark, including the Wright Brothers National Memorial, all the way up to Montreal, Canada, where we took in the 1976 Olympics. With the kids getting better using the CB trucker's lingo, we headed to Toronto and then south, seeing Niagara Falls among other sights on the way home. Our month-long journey was a history and geography lesson we treasure.

The next summer, 1977, when Johnny got his learner's license, the three of us took our camper on a six-week trip out West, as far as Washington State. I had spent months of planning so that we saw many national parks and visited my sister and her family in Oregon, on a big loop around the United States. With Johnny at the wheel doing most of the driving, I was the backseat driver. Since experience is the best teacher, and my suggestions were usually too little too late, I simply offered observations such as "Johnny, you shouldn't make a swift U-turn in the middle of traffic just because the navigator thought we were going the wrong way." Jeffrey was the map reader and navigator. While he honed his directional skills (which are quite good today, you'll be glad to know), I was looking out the window and asking, "Where did you say we are?"

Each of us took turns cooking and cleaning up at the campgrounds. That meant I cooked a third of the time. Whoever was the cook also did the shopping for food. I gave some basic nutrition advice then tried not to interfere with their menu choices. Did you know you can lose weight on peanut butter and jelly sandwiches if you eat them for two-thirds of your meals?

As for school, well, I would love to have some of Jeff's teachers see him now! From the first grade and into high school, I was regularly summoned to teacher conferences. All Jeff's elementary teachers admitted that he wouldn't have gotten away with it if he weren't so cute! The "it" could be anything a rambunctious boy could think up that did not involve schoolwork. As he got older, it was just the schoolwork that was the problem. That turned out to be a big problem when he took the college preadmittance exam. His scores were such that we had to pay for him to go to summer school before he could be accepted into the university. One of the courses was English. I cannot believe I am writing this now in a book *he* has written!

Over the years, Jeff has told me about his flying adventures and misadventures. It is fun, scary, and amazing to recall those stories as I now read about them in this book. I remember feeling a bit fearful when he told me about hitting the tree tops, hanging up-side-down on the beach and such, but I didn't worry because he did tell me. He even told me, but I don't think he told you, about his high school prank, rolling the high school football field. For anyone not familiar with teenagers, "rolling" is throwing, or in this case *dropping*, rolls of toilet paper to *decorate* an area. He was caught because the toilet paper—hanging from the floodlights surrounding the field—obviously couldn't have been thrown up there; they must have been dropped from an airplane. He was the only high school pilot. I don't believe I heard that story right away; I think it was a couple years later when he told me. Now you know, too.

Jeff has told you about learning to fly during those years and how ROTC changed his life's direction. He didn't tell you that I was his first passenger when he got his pilot's license at 17. It was quite windy that day, and he slipped the plane a bit sideways as we landed, looking completely at ease and professional. Although a bit anxious, I trusted his knowledge and expertise then just as I trusted him driving our car and trust him in his decisions today.

That is the not very colorful story of our growing-up years. I say "our" because the three of us did grow and learn together. I did what millions of parents do: I raised two wonderful children through some difficult times and some great times. We had the support of our family and friends and the unconditional love and wisdom of my parents, to whom I owe my stability. My little boys grew into young men and set out to make their own way in the world. I believe you can get an idea, from this brief history, how Jeff's early family life has influenced him. And now they were young adults.

Jeff has told you a bit about how Johnny struggled with alcohol. He was about 26 and living on his own when his problems reached a crisis. I was working on my master's degree in school guidance counseling and happened to be taking a class on addictions. With that knowledge and divine intervention, I was able to get him into a month-long hospital addiction program, and it worked. We watched him grow up into the fine young man we knew he was. He passed the rigorous Florida general contractor exam on the first try and obtained his license. He married and became a devoted father and able provider.

Jeff was stationed near Fairbanks, Alaska, flying the A-10, when Joellen was born, my first grandchild. That summer, when she was 6 months old, I flew out to visit her—and her parents, too, of course. Jeff rented a camper and took his little family, including me, for a grand tour of Alaska. It reminded me of our trips not so many years before, except this time Jeff got to do the driving. Less than a year later, with Jeff stationed back in the lower 48, Michael followed close after Joellen, almost as close as Johnny and Jeffrey.

Jeff was now "Odie" to his air force buddies but he was still Jeff to us and growing into his role as a parent and a provider. When he left the military, he sought other flying jobs because that was his passion.

You will recall that while my two boys were becoming young men, they had a half brother who was also growing up, unknown to us. At about the same time we lost Johnny, Sean lost his younger brother, Christian. Sean for some time had wanted to know who his real father was, and, at last, his mother told him. You know the story. When Jeff called me with "Guess what, Mom!" I was not surprised; I was thrilled. Jeffrey had a brother again! What an amazing blessing! And when Sean came with Jeff to meet me and our family, it was a homecoming. I laughed and told them I thought that Johnny and Christian had gotten together in heaven and decided that their brothers down here needed each other, so they arranged it. Now, I consider Sean to be mine, too.

I am retired now, but during my working years, my grandchildren were growing up and I saw them every chance I could. During the summers, for a week to 10 days, Jeffrey's two children were sent from Georgia and Johnny's two from a couple hours north of me, and "Camp Grandma" was in session. I spent many hours planning ahead for activities and excursions to keep them busy every minute. We enjoyed those summer get-togethers until they grew up and activities at home took all their time. Yet today, the four cousins remain close, I believe as a result of those yearly times of play together.

How did Jeff come to where he is now? Becoming what he describes as a Target Leader has been a process, an evolution. He reads, he listens, he remembers, and he thinks. With a smile I can say he has changed from little fun-loving Jeffrey to big fun-loving Odie. Jeff's innate sense of humor and his sense of seeing the positive side of life, coupled with the discipline of his military and commercial pilot training, have imbued him with the ability to impart wisdom in a memorable way. Yet, there is more. There is a passion and a fire.

That comes from Johnny. That tragic April day, 1995, changed us all, and for Jeff, it ignited a smoldering fire into a bright flame. His brother's loss could have grown and consumed him, but he slowly took control and let it build into a positive energy for Johnny's sake and in Johnny's memory. I cannot take credit for the evolution of the Odie you hear at the speaker's stand and who wrote this book. I have watched in wonder as this man evolves. I understand the grief he felt when we lost Johnny and the passion he feels in trying to prevent other families from knowing this grief. Jeff believes passionately that accidents can be prevented, and I concur absolutely. What Jeff has done with that tragedy, turning it into a zeal, a passion, a determination to prevent accidents that devastate lives, has been his own.

I do not believe that Jeff's actions or instructions to his brother had anything to do with the accident that took the life of our Johnny and their friend, Craig. At the same time, I can accept that a preventable oversight may have caused the accident that day, and for the sake of the lesson in safety, I will accept that possibility. There is never a good reason to be slack when safety is at stake. As for me, I understand that God, in his wisdom, took Johnny. The great thing is that I got to have him, know him, and love him for almost 33 years. He left me two wonderful grandsons. Zachary is in college and learning to fly. Alan is in high school and is an outstanding baseball player.

I must mention here that being a grandmother again, 20 years after my first grandchild was born, has been an indescribable joy. With Kai, everything is new; everything is possible. I love seeing the world in and through his eyes.

Let's keep that sense of wonder and remember how precious life is. Let's make safety our priority as we work and play. Let's remember and use the principles Jeff has set forth in this book. Nothing here is new, just said in a different way—a way that we hope you will understand, accept, remember, and apply in your work and home.

ABOUT THE AUTHOR

J eff "Odie" Espenship is a former USAF A-10 Warthog fighter pilot and current international airline pilot. He is also the founder of Target Leadership, a company that focuses on motivating employees at all levels to embrace their organizations' policies and procedures. Odie's inspirational message is one of the most sought-after keynotes among the nation's Fortune 100 and 500 corporations. He inspires behavior changes and emphasizes a zero-accident safety culture among all employees. Odie's leadership-safety-culture DVDs are also sold worldwide in several languages.